A STILL, SMALL VOICE

FR. BENEDICT J. GROESCHEL, C.F.R.

A STILL, SMALL VOICE

A Practical Guide on Reported Revelations

"And after the fire there was a still, small voice."
—1 Kings 19:12

"To ecstasy, I prefer the monotony of sacrifice."
—Saint Thérèse of Lisieux

IGNATIUS PRESS   SAN FRANCISCO

Nihil Obstat: James T. O'Connor, S.T.D.
                Censor Librorum

Imprimatur: † Patrick Sheridan, D.D.
                Vicar General
                Archdiocese of New York
                November 30, 1992

Cover art: *St. Thérèse of Lisieux* by John Lynch
Cover design by Riz Boncan Marsella

*This book is gratefully dedicated
to the many cloistered
religious, nuns, and monks
in English-speaking countries
who have so generously supported
my work and the Franciscans of the Renewal
with their vigils, prayers, and
the monotony of their sacrifices.*

CONTENTS

ACKNOWLEDGMENTS

I am deeply grateful to the following friends who have helped so generously in making this book possible. As he has often done in the past, Charles Prendegast has corrected the manuscript and made many helpful suggestions, both as to style and content. Father Bernard Panczuk, O.S.B.M., provincial of the Basilian Monks, and Father Eugene Fulton, director of Trinity Retreat, have very kindly checked the manuscript. Elaine Barone has patiently done all the typing, and John Lynch has provided another of his fine paintings for the cover art. He has captured both the mysticism and struggles of Saint Thérèse of Lisieux, whose simple insight has been so helpful in this matter of private revelation. I am also grateful to so many of my teachers and students who have shared their religious experiences with me over the years.

—Fr. Benedict Joseph Groeschel, C.F.R.
St. Crispin's Friary, Bronx, New York
Feast of the Sacred Heart of Jesus, 1992

9

INTRODUCTION

A Practical Guide

This book is meant to be a practical guide for those interested in private revelations and in reports of visions and other extraordinary religious phenomena. This interest may be personal, arising from one's own experience or from deep spiritual interest in the reports of others. The reader's interest may also be more objective, arising from a legitimate curiosity or from a desire to help by guiding those who find themselves in these deep waters. Many readers have been profoundly influenced all their lives by the extraordinary experiences and visions of Saint Francis, Saint Teresa of Avila, or by Saint Margaret Mary's mystical image of the Sacred Heart of Jesus. Few Catholics can claim honestly that they have not been influenced by the experience of Saint Bernadette at Lourdes.

At the present time there is a completely unexpected and incredibly diverse interest in what the psychologists of religion would call paranormal or paramystical phenomena. Bishops and priests, counselors and therapists, superiors and pastors, Protestant clergy and people in the media, and even relatives and friends are likely to be called upon to make a judgment or give an opinion on experiences that range from Medjugorje to the New Age. This book is meant to be a brief but comprehensive guide to all these inquirers and to open doors for those who feel that they need to know more.

My interest is both personal and objective. I have visited shrines and holy places, beginning with the Holy Land, and I have been gratefully filled with the pilgrim's joy and fervor. I have also counseled some of those involved in questionable revelations, interviewed seers, and met skeptics turned ardent believers. I have even known a brilliant psychologist who in all innocence was the recipient of a false revelation.

For a number of years I have been working on a larger and more comprehensive book on the psychology of religious experience. In it I intend to review many studies of all kinds of religious phenomena. However, the intense interest in extraordinary religious experience at the present time has made me see that a concise practical book is urgently needed now. This is a bit of enlightened self-interest on my part. I need something to save time when serious people earnestly, almost desperately, ask questions about what is happening to them and their friends. Candidly, I need to be able to hand someone a book. While not a comprehensive study of private revelation, this book will be, I hope, a helpful guide to the devout, the responsible, and even the merely curious.

A Review of Information Not Easily Available

For the most part, this book does not contain original material. It is derived from spiritual classics and from documents that are not readily available. I have drawn much from the standard work, *The Graces of Interior Prayer* by Father Augustin Poulain, S. J. This monumental study was first published in 1901 and went through at least ten editions up to 1922.[1] Anyone more seriously interested in alleged private revelations must study this great work, which was written at a time like our own when, in the doldrums of materialism and rationalism, a profound reaction caused a wide but often misguided interest in paranormal phenomena, some religious, some related to the psychic, and some magical. Evelyn Underhill, a spiritual writer of those times, called the magical "a feeble, a deformed or an arrogant mystical sense".[2]

Does God Speak Now?

Despite all the humbug arising from what is termed the New Age movement on the one hand, and the religious hype giving rise to endless reports of appearances of the Blessed Virgin on the other, an intelligent person who is not terrified by the unknown should be interested in something that elicits such widespread interest. A person concerned with his own spiritual life should be aware that "God has visited his people" throughout the ages, beginning with the prophets and continuing down through the history of the Church. These visitations do not add to the single, unique, and complete message of the Messiah, but apply and, as it were, highlight certain aspects of his teaching in different times and circumstances. In Christ are all the treasures of wisdom and knowledge (cf. Col 2:3), but he did send apostles like Peter and Paul to deliver this message with their own

[1] Augustin Poulain, S. J., *The Graces of Interior Prayer* (London: Routledge and Kegan Paul, 1950).

[2] Evelyn Underhill, *Mysticism,* rev. ed. (New York: New American Library, 1974).

particular gifts. Can he not speak now through seers and even through others like creative teachers to renew the impact of the gospel? However, to make one's way through the confusing possibilities, to sort out all the subjective elements that individuals inevitably add, to discard the rubbish, to dismiss kindly those who with the best of intentions have been misled, and to filter out what is, in fact, a grace of God—all this is no small task.

An Alternative to Ecstasy

In my final chapter I offer an alternative to unusual and extraordinary ways of knowing the things of God. There is a normal, everyday opportunity open to those who seek God, called religious experience. This is the action of grace operating in the context of a human life. If we allow it, grace will elicit deeply-moving responses and become a powerful source of virtue. This is the meaning of the words of Saint Thérèse of Lisieux:

"To ecstasy, I prefer the monotony of sacrifice."

Notice she does not use the passive verb "accept". She *prefers* the plain fulfillment of one's duties. The active reception of the innumerable signs of grace that surround us, the faithful carrying out of responsibilities, and the willingness to work on daily repentance make a symphony of religious experience, which is appreciated by those who are willing to take the time and make the effort. Perhaps many who are clinging to or seeking the reassurances given by extraordinary experience might be much better off if they knew how to grow and be enriched by the ordinary experience of God and the Holy which are available to all. Saint John of the Cross, the mystical Doctor of the Church, who warned people to assume that extraordinary experiences came from the forces of evil unless the opposite could be proved, would enthusiastically agree.

An appreciation of and sensitivity to ordinary religious experience frees a person from the possibility of serious error and spiritual pride. Thérèse of Lisieux hardly ever had extraordinary experiences, and yet her life was filled with a profound awareness of the presence of Divine Love. She even regarded falling asleep at her prayers as religious experience. The monotony of sacrifice, fidelity, and generosity may be the safest and most productive of all religious experience, and it is there waiting for us all.

One

PRIVATE REVELATIONS—
IN THIS DAY AND AGE

An astonishing degree of attention is paid in these unbelieving times to revelations apparently made to ordinary people by the Lord himself, the Blessed Virgin Mary, or other messengers from the world unknown to our earthly senses. These communications, or, as they are properly called, private revelations, attract immense interest not only from Catholic and Orthodox Christians but from Protestants, from people in the media, unbelievers, and more scientists than those who are willing to admit it publicly. Inquiries about these things come not only from the devout who are familiar with such revelations as the Sacred Heart of Christ or Our Lady of Lourdes, but also from apparently religiously uninvolved people who may be looking for help with some overwhelming problem or illness, or from reporters just looking for a story. Interest on the part of those in academia was just recently highlighted by a serious study of Marian apparitions by Sandra Zimdars-Swartz,[1] a professor at the University of Kansas.

[1] Sandra Zimdars-Swartz, *Encountering Mary* (Princeton, N.J.: Princeton University Press, 1991).

Reports of weeping Madonnas, miraculous physical cures, prophecies, and heavenly warnings generally leave members of the clergy annoyed, perplexed, and skeptical. This is because so often the news of these events, real or imagined, is delivered by people who are seen as easily excitable or a bit unbalanced. Because these events rarely happen to the clergy, who are terrified of being seen as superstitious or credulous, the average priest or minister will plead ignorance of such things, while rabbis will be grateful that these events are almost unknown in the Jewish world outside of Hasidism. Many of the clergy hoped and thought that such religious phenomena belonged to another time and were glad to leave them there. However, a review of popular religious literature will reveal that there is not only a growing involvement in private revelations by the devout, but also a revival of interest in the psychic and pseudo-mystical by sophisticated types who have for the moment given up traditional religion in favor of the vagaries of the New Age. Incredibly, those who would scoff at a prayerful visit to the Blessed Sacrament may be seen walking around affluent neighborhoods in New York, London, Paris, and Berlin communicating with the psychic powers using their own pocket crystal. So much for the inroads of scientific skepticism. Only the clergy seem to be universally affected by it.

While I suspect that few of my readers are involved with the New Age religion, many are wondering what it's all about when a real estate agent or an accountant fasts on bread and water on Wednesday because Our Lady suggested this penance at Medjugorje. What does it mean when reports of Marian apparitions are passed on by a Protestant evangelist who is convinced that Mary is indeed appearing to young Croatians in a mountain village? How do you react when your favorite priest lets you know that a devout colleague in Italy heard from Our Lady that she was not pleased with the new look in the Church? Are these communications to be accepted as a new revelation, a fifth Gospel, a postscript to the New Testament? Or are they all nonsense and superstition? Do they reflect a desperate need for certitude occasioned by the shallowness and confusion of contemporary religious teaching and preaching?

The question becomes more insistent when one considers the history of private revelation. Is there something to be learned from the fact that an eminent scientist and Nobel Prize winner, Alexis Carrel, was converted from militant atheism at Lourdes? Should we be interested that the Pope returned to pray at Fatima only recently? It is worth mentioning that at least one private revelation—that given to Saint Margaret Mary—has left the Catholic landscape dotted with churches, hospitals, and universities named after the Sacred Heart. People claiming private revelations outside the Catholic ambience present even more intriguing questions. Among others the Mormons and the Seventh-Day Adventists owe their entire existence as denominations to claims of private revelation made by very serious people. Writers and musicians as different as Taylor Caldwell and George Frederick Handel have more than hinted that they were assisted by heavenly powers in their creative work. When I was a student at Columbia University, I studied under a psychologist, Helen Schucman, who considered herself an agnostic until one day she began writing what some have seen as a private revelation—the so-called *Course in Miracles,* about which we will say more.

Unfortunately, people unfamiliar with real or alleged private revelations can be literally blown off course by such phenomena and change their whole lives in response to them, because they do not have any tools for assessing alleged revelations and sorting out their own possible responses. When one considers the immense labors of the Mormons in response to the reported revelations of Joseph Smith or the devotion of the members of the Bahai faith to the teachings of their prophet, one might feel a pinch of gratitude toward the mainstream clergy for their studied diffidence toward claims of supernatural knowledge. At least their diffidence causes those involved in alleged revelations to proceed slowly and carefully.

Many of those who are enthusiastic about the reported apparitions at Medjugorje are horrified by the strong disapproval of the local bishop. In the face of much criticism, the bishop of Mostar has held that these experiences are not authentic signs from God. Whether these revelations eventually are accepted or rejected by the Church, the bishop's attitude honestly and consistently expressed is an important ingredient in the whole story. If these alleged revelations are ultimately accepted as probably authentic (the most the Church can do), then his suspicions will add to their credibility. If, on the other hand, they are rejected, he will have saved the Church from much embarrassment. In such a complex situation it is surprising to find someone in such a no-lose situation. The worst that can happen is that eventually the bishop may have to make some apologies to the

Virgin Mary—but then we have it on the best authority that she is very benevolent and understanding. One might assume that with a couple of Rosaries the bishop will be out of trouble with the Blessed Mother. My problem with the bishop and his advisors, as well as with everyone else except the visionaries themselves, is that they are all so sure of their respective positions. The visionaries have at least a subjective excuse for being certain. I had the opportunity to interview one of the young visionaries, Maria Paprovick, for over an hour, through an interpreter. I found her to be a rather level-headed, sensible peasant girl. Without clear evidence of fraud or mental illness, how can anyone else be so certain in completely rejecting their accounts? This observation introduces the next question, namely, are there coherent rules for the evaluation of reports of revelations?

Two

KEEPING A PERSPECTIVE

I am often asked the question, "Are there some rules for coping with private revelations?" As a matter of fact there are well thought-out rules to guide the person interested in private revelation—rules that have been formulated over the centuries not only by serious spiritual directors and students of mystical phenomena but also by the popes. Some norms were devised by those who were very familiar with direct experience from above, like Saint Teresa and Saint John of the Cross. Other rules came from people who had carefully studied the accounts of those who claim to have had experiences. As already indicated, I am especially indebted in this writing to Father Augustin Poulain, S. J., author of the classic in this field, *The Graces of Interior Prayer.* Unfortunately, this book, written ninety years ago, is not easily available and is composed in a style different from our own. Those familiar with this kind of literature will do well to consult Poulain's work, which is available in any adequate Catholic library.

To make things easier for the general reader, I will simply state norms that are drawn partly from Poulain and partly synthesized from classical writers. I will explain these rules as briefly as possible.

Rule 1. *Keep all claims of revelations in perspective.*

Private revelations are not the most important things in the world. The consistent and authentic pursuit of a holy life leading to a loving union with God is the essential element of true religion. Many great saints reported no unusual experiences at all. Among eminent nonvisionaries in our own century are Saint Thérèse of Lisieux and Saint Maximilian Kolbe.

It is important to keep clearly in mind that private revelations have no significance apart from the public revelation of Sacred Scripture, interpreted by the traditional teaching of the Church. This principle was reiterated by Pope John Paul II as recently as 1983. While on a pilgrimage to Fatima the Holy Father said:

> The Church has always taught and continues to proclaim that God's revelation was brought to completion in Jesus Christ, who is the fullness of that revelation, and that "no new public revelation is to be expected before the glorious manifestation of our Lord" (*Dei Verbum* 4). The Church evaluates and judges private revelations by the criterion of conformity with that single Revelation.
>
> If the Church has accepted the message of Fatima, it is above all because the message contains a truth and a call whose basic content is the truth and the call of the Gospel itself.[1]

This public revelation is available to all. It is most important to keep this truth in mind. Do you want to know the certain and direct revelation of God? Pick up a Bible and read it! Do you want to be speedily and mysteriously in the presence of Christ? Reverently and prayerfully visit the Blessed Sacrament! Do

[1] Cited in George Kosicki, C.S.B., *Now Is the Time for Mercy* (Steubenville, Oh.: Franciscan University Press, 1991), 70.

you want to see and touch Jesus Christ? Serve the poor! These means are available to all, and they are incontrovertibly true.

One may then legitimately ask: Why do we have private revelations at all? The obvious reply is: "Ask God." True revelations, public or private, are never contrived or planned by human beings. They happen as the result of causes beyond human control or knowledge. Public revelation is given to the people of God in Scripture and is addressed to all for all times. It must be accepted and believed. Public revelation in this precise sense ended with the close of the apostolic age.

The end of public revelation does not at all mean that God no longer reveals himself to his children. He continues to do so, but now indirectly or in what we call private revelations, as well as by other means of his Divine Providence. Karl Rahner gives the following helpful explanation of the distinction between public and private revelations.

> The tradition and practice of the Church (in devotions, prophetic figures in the Church, acknowledged mystics) presuppose the existence of genuine private revelation. Then again, the "closing" of (public) revelation ("since the death of the apostles") must not be taken to mean that since then, in contrast to former times, the attitude of God to individual and collective history is silent and aloof. The "closing" of revelation indicates the absolute supremacy and permanent normative character of the Christ-event, which remains to produce new fruits of the Spirit in the Church.[2]

Private revelation is possible for the same reasons that public revelation is possible: the Divine Being

---

[2] Karl Rahner, *Sacramentum Mundi,* vol. 5 (New York: Herder and Herder, 1970), 358ff.

can and does communicate with limited created beings. Private revelation may be said to encourage or even to guide individuals or the whole Church at a particular time. It is my opinion that most private revelations are unknown to others. God's specific calls and challenges, as well as his individual guidance usually remain completely unknown, except to the one to whom they are addressed. Sometimes, however, revelations are given to individuals to be shared. Saint Bernadette made known the message and promise she received, and indeed a great shrine came into existence as a result. Sometimes a private revelation may alter the events of history, as did the call of Saint Joan of Arc, who in a single year changed the course of European history to this day. Saint Catherine of Siena, following personal inspirations she received, called Pope Gregory XI back from Avignon and preserved the sovereignty of the papacy from royal domination. It is obvious, then, that we cannot deny the possibility or the lasting effects of God's communication with certain individuals, even though the public revelation was completed nineteen hundred years ago. However, to maintain a proper perspective, it is wise to recall that for Catherine, Joan, and Bernadette personally, these powerful revelations were only incidents along the way of their short and eventful lives. The essential thing in each case was that these young women had unwavering faith and love and sought to do the will of God and to follow the path marked out in the gospel by Christ for all who wish to be saved. They were not merely visionaries; they were saints.

Three

TRUTH AND PRIVATE REVELATIONS

It is the teaching of the Church that public revelation is true and, when properly understood, without error. Can the same thing be said about private revelation? We often assume that the same verity we ascribe to the Bible exists in the private revelation that is approved. This brings us to a very important principle.

Rule 2. *No private revelation comes directly from God and therefore none can be assumed to be inerrantly true.*

A firm grasp of this fact could shed a great deal of light on the present discussion of particular private revelations. For centuries it has been a clear papal teaching that even a canonized saint who has reported a private revelation which has been approved by the Church for acceptance by the faithful may have introduced some personal element that is subject to error or distortion. This fact is not sufficiently well known. If you are interested in private revelations, learning this principle is worth all the time and effort that it has taken to read this book so far. The converse is also true, namely, that because a visionary may have erred in the report of a revelation, one cannot conclude that this person has not received a special grace. He or she may have distorted the revelation unconsciously. It is also true that if visionaries proclaim prophecy which turns out to be correct, one cannot by that fact alone assume that they received the revelation from God. They may, in fact, have gained the knowledge in some other way.

Pope Benedict XIV, writing about the partially approved revelations of Saint Hildegard (who gets much attention today from New Age devotees), of Saint Bridget, and of Saint Catherine of Siena taught authoritatively:

> "What is to be said of those private revelations which the Apostolic See has *approved* of, those of the Blessed Hildegard (which were approved in part by Eugene III), of St. Bridget [by Boniface IX], and of St. Catherine of Siena [by Gregory XI]? We have already said that those revelations, although approved of, ought not to, and cannot, receive from us any assent of Catholic, but only of *human faith,* according to the rules of prudence, according to which the aforesaid revelations are *probable,* and *piously to be believed (probabiles et pie credibiles)"* (*De canon.,* book III, chap. liii, no. 15; book II, chap. xxxii, no. 11. Eng. trans: Benedict XIV on Heroic Virtue, vol. III, chap. xiv).[1]

It is essential to grasp the distinction that the Pope makes between Catholic faith relating to the theological virtue (the faith with which we believe in public revelation, as, for example, in the Creed) and human faith, by which we believe in the democratic way of life or that someone loves us. When I am asked if I believe in a particular private revelation (even my favorite, Lourdes), I always reply that I

---

[1] A. Poulain, *Graces of Interior Prayer* (London: Routledge and Kegan Paul, 1950), 320.

believe in the Catholic Christian Faith and I *think* that Lourdes is a special gift of God to us all. Although I have a very strong opinion as to the validity of Bernadette's testimony, I would be wrong to say I believe in the Lourdes phenomena with theological faith. It is quite possible, even in a revelation which has received Church approval, that one can be misled. Consequently, according to Benedict XIV, we can give these revelations only prudent acceptance as probable.

Several questions should arise immediately in the minds of those interested in private revelations: "How can there be error? How can this be? How can a vision from God be wrong?" It cannot. But the recipient of the vision can make mistakes. No divine revelation is immediately received by a visionary. It is filtered through the perceptive faculties of the human being who receives it. Here an old Latin proverb is pertinent: "That which is received is received in the manner of the receiver." A good analogy often used is light passing through a glass prism. The prism causes a distortion in our perception of the pure white light, a rainbow distortion that may be beautiful and helpful. But don't try driving a car with a prism before your eyes.

In the strictest sense of the word, the only complete direct revelation of God came through the Divine Person of Our Lord Jesus Christ. He alone has known the Father as he is (Jn 14:8–11). Beyond this, faith tells us that the entire public revelation is kept free from substantive distortion by the power of the Holy Spirit. However, if you are familiar enough with the Epistles, you can see that the different personal traits of the writers are reflected in the public revelation that came through them. Paul is a very different person from James, and both from the Johannine writer. All of these New Testament writers were guided, and their works must be accepted as part of public revelation. The same cannot be assumed to be true of Saint Catherine of Siena or Saint Teresa of Avila, although both have great authority based on their position in the Church as Doctors and on their own perceptive observations on the spiritual life. Our respect may call forth an assent of what Pope Benedict XIV calls human faith, but which we are more likely to refer to as strong opinion in the language of our time.

Does this mean that you do not have to believe that Our Lady appeared at Lourdes to Bernadette? As someone deeply devoted to this shrine and to Saint Bernadette and as one who has a very strong opinion that it all happened as the little peasant saint said, it pains me to admit that you do not have to accept the apparition at Lourdes if, after studying the facts, you decide not to. (I reserve the right to think you are foolish if you don't.)

What about the papal encyclicals on the Sacred Heart? A reading of any of these profound documents, including the most recent, *Haurietis Aquas,* written Pope Pius XII in 1956, will demonstrate that the popes as well as theologians do not derive their teaching from private revelations but from Scripture and theology.[2] The several encyclicals over the centuries avoid all but the most circumspect mention of the revelations to Saint Margaret Mary Alacoque in the seventeenth century. However, it will be everlastingly to the credit of this humble and saintly soul

[2] Jan Bovenmars, M.S.C., *Biblical Spirituality of the Heart* (New York: Alba House, 1991), 179ff.

that she was the occasion of this particular train of thought in theology, and what is more important, she was the providential instrument of a devotion that has brought hundreds of millions of people closer to the love of the Son of God symbolized by his Sacred Heart.[3]

The reasons for possible mistakes and distortions in revelations are many, and we shall review them separately. However, it is necessary before doing so to point out that all authentic private revelations are responses of a specific individual in a very concrete historical situation to a divine call—a theophany—the adequate knowledge of which is ultimately beyond all limitations of our senses or intelligence. If you will, it is the Infinite Reality trying to communicate with a finite being. Beyond this difficulty, there is the basic fact that with human knowledge every perception of things outside one's own inner being has some distortion in it due to previous experience and expectations of the individual. We all have our own frames of reference, which in psychology are referred to by the German word *Gestalten*. An example may help us to appreciate this important fact. A woman may bring her young daughter to a great performance of the opera *Madama Butterfly*. The mother is deeply moved by an artistically powerful production of this familiar story. The child may be bored by everything but the stage scenery. They have different frames of reference and perceive the same reality on stage in very different ways by reason of what they think is important and attractive. The

[3] Timothy O'Donnell, *Heart of the Redeemer* (San Francisco: Ignatius Press, 1992). See chapter 4 for a review of papal teaching.

same effect is true of the frame of reference in a mystical vision associated with a private revelation. It is reported that a Mexican Indian, Blessed Juan Diego, tried to avoid the beautiful lady who spoke to him at Guadalupe and who told him she was his Mother.[4] Bernadette admired the beautiful young woman she saw, but initially had no idea that it was an apparition of Our Lady.[5] On the other hand, Saint Margaret Mary was informed and perceptive enough to realize immediately that she was seeing a vision of the Savior. Rahner sums up this effect of different *Gestalten* in the following perceptive if complex quotation.

> Any given private revelation is always—as experience shows, in Scripture and in the Church—a synthesis in which the character of the recipient, as determined historically (theologically, culturally, etc.) and psychologically (or para-psychologically), is fused with the mystical or normal grace given to him in the depths of his existence. Hence one cannot exclude the possibility of illusions, misinterpretations and distortions, even where there is genuine private revelation according to the ordinary criteria by which mystical phenomena are judged. In particular, the "visionary" element in private revelations has in fact very clearly a "contemporary style". The "genuineness" of a private revelation is a very variable quantity.[6]

Because authentic private revelations are so related to the particular situation of the individual, the Church does not use them, nor should we generally

[4] Sr. M. Amatora, W.S.F., *The Queen's Portrait* (Academy Press, Fresno, Calif.: 1961), 106.

[5] René Laurentin, *Bernadette of Lourdes* (Minneapolis: Winston Press, 1979), 27–32.

[6] Karl Rahner, *Sacramentum Mundi,* vol. 5 (New York: Herder and Herder, 1970), 358.

use them, to decide matters with little or no relationship to the revelation or message itself.

This principle was very well summed up by Cardinal Pitra, quoted by Poulain.

> Everyone knows that we are fully at liberty to believe or not to believe in private revelations, even those most worthy of credence. Even when the Church *approves* them, they are merely received as *probable,* and not as indubitable. They are not to be used as *deciding questions* of history, natural philosophy, philosophy, or theology which are matters of controversy between the Doctors. It is quite permissible to differ from these revelations, even when approved, if we are relying upon solid reasons, and especially if the contrary doctrine is proved by unimpeachable documents and definite experience (Book on St. Hildegard, p. xvi).[7]

The personal character of private revelations and especially the fact that they are deeply influenced by the subjectivity of the individual require that their use be very circumscribed and generally limited to the situation in which the revelation occurred. It is difficult to express these limitations in a single statement because the applications will vary and also because of the ongoing persistent possibility of distortion.

Some private revelations were apparently meant to have a wide circulation and effect. For example, the request made to Bernadette for the building of a church at the grotto. Apparently a revelation destined to have far-reaching effect was received by the three children of Fatima. They reported the revelations with the same direct naïveté that characterized the statements of Bernadette. As far as one can tell, no attempt has ever been made by the papal diplomatic

[7] Poulain, *Graces of Interior Prayer,* 320–21.

corps, or much less by any government, to determine policy on the basis of these revelations. That would have been beyond their purpose. It seems to me post factum that one may speculate about the relationships of these revelations to the astonishingly rapid collapse of Communism and to the religious revival in Russia indicated by these children who had no knowledge of world history or geography. They reported the Virgin Mary's request that the Rosary be widely recited throughout the world so that many people would be led to penance and prayer for world peace and especially for the conversion of Russia.[8]

The question arises: Why try to make limitations on revelations? An example may answer this question. Saint Catherine Labouré, who gave the world the miraculous medal, actually predicted the bloody disturbances of the French Commune forty years before they occurred and with the precise date.[9] However, she made several other predictions that were wrong. When confronted with these errors, she simply apologized for getting the facts of the revelation wrong. She obviously did not know what to say, since she thought she had got the message right.[10] This admission of simply "getting it wrong" on the part of this simple visionary is something one should never forget.

[8] Cf. Sandra Zimdars-Swartz, *Encountering Mary* (Princeton, N.J.: Princeton University Press, 1991), 198ff., for a careful description of the secrets and of the memoirs of Sr. Lucia.

[9] Poulain, *Graces of Interior Prayer,* 330.

[10] Ibid., 330.

Four

THE SCOPE OF PRIVATE REVELATIONS

Because error so often occurs in private revelation, it is necessary to try to develop some general principle for applying knowledge from private revelation to the lives of others outside the direct circumstances. Certainly some revelations were meant for more than one time and for more than a small circle of people. Some revelations changed world history, and some contributed to the shape of spirituality in the Church. I suggest a general principle requiring careful application may be formulated in the following way.

Rule 3. *A private revelation by definition is personal and therefore must be carefully applied by those for whom it was meant and only within the limits of ordinary human prudence and never in an unreasonable way or against the teaching of the Church. It must never be considered an infallible guide in any situation.*

It may be difficult to determine how far the knowledge of a private revelation should be disseminated. Is it perhaps meant to be generally known throughout the Church? It is obvious that no private revelation can bind everyone, because it is expressly taught by the Church that no one is required to accept a private revelation. There have been a number of revelations in modern times, apparently addressed to the faithful in a general way, for example, the messages of Fatima. It is easy to establish that no Catholic is obliged to accept such a popular revelation from the following facts. In the process of beatification, in which a comprehensive examination is made of the consistent and heroic virtue of the individual in following the gospel teachings, no account is ever taken as to whether the servants of God have adhered to or even accepted such widely addressed revelations. It would be completely inconsistent with the procedures of the Church to ask a question like this: "Did the Servant of God, so-and-so, follow the devotions called for by Our Lady at Fatima?" Therefore it logically follows that no one can admonish another person for not following a private revelation. The refusal to accept the revelation may reveal attitudes of unbelief or worldliness which are spiritually unsound. But the simple decision not to take account of a private revelation in one's own life is acceptable, although a truly devoted person would tend to take an authenticated revelation very seriously (with human faith).

It is also worth noting that because one believes that a revelation is from God, one is not thereby dispensed from following legitimate ecclesiastical authority. Revelations do not make or dispense from Church laws. A revelation that did so would be certainly suspect. On the other hand, it is important to realize that ecclesiastical authority itself is obviously limited by certain parameters, such as the need to back up decisions with evidence. Authorities can, for good reason, state the opinion that the alleged revelations are contrary to faith or perhaps suggest mental imbalance on the part of visionaries. Competent authority may exercise some control of the expressions of piety surrounding a revelation, and this has often been done. As Zimdars-Swartz has so well documented, there is a difference between the diffidence and distance of the ecclesiastical authorities concerning a reported revelation and condemnation of it. There are several cases where ecclesiastical authorities went from attitudes of suspicion and outright rejection to acceptance of the revelation and support of its message. A perfect example is the Abbé Peyramale, the parish priest of Saint Peter's in Lourdes, who went from being a complete skeptic as regards Bernadette's testimony to being one of her staunchest supporters.[1]

We will now move to the discussion of errors made in understanding or communicating revelations, by those who have received them.

[1] L. Von Matt, *Bernadette of Lourdes* (New York: Universe Books, 1963).

Five

REVELATIONS—AUTHENTIC, QUESTIONABLE, FALSE, AND FAKE

Before moving to our fourth principle pertaining to errors made in reporting genuine revelations, we need to make some distinctions. For the purpose of our discussion I will refer to those revelations as authentic which have been approved by the Church as probably being extraordinary divine manifestations. Many reported revelations are still under consideration or in dispute, and I will refer to these as questionable. A false revelation is one which the recipient believes to be supernatural but is not. A fake revelation is simply the ruse of a charlatan. These distinctions need further clarification.

Authentic Revelations

A revelation or vision may be approved in a variety of ways and degrees. The simplest way is a decision by the diocesan commission promulgated by the local bishop saying that after all the facts have been studied, the revelations can be accepted as probable. Usually this is done after the death of the visionary. Visitors to Lourdes are familiar with the monument showing the decree of Bishop Laurence of Tarbes, which states that there is no reason to believe that these events reported by Bernadette did not occur and approves the devotion of the faithful. This decree was dated January 18, 1862, eighteen years before the death of Saint Bernadette on April 16, 1879.

A less formal approval comes from the devout visits of many distinguished clergy and laity over a period of time. Obviously the strongest approval of this kind would come from a papal visit. The establishment of a universal liturgical feast (by papal authority) is also a strong approbation whereas a local or informal feast may bring a less impressive but recognizable approval.

Questionable Revelations

Questionable revelations obviously are far more numerous than approved ones. Father P. Deletter, S. J., a theologian who wrote extensively on this subject, states that twenty-two Marian apparitions were seriously studied between 1931 and 1950, and only two were approved (Beauraing and Banneaux, in Belgium). Six remained undecided in 1952 and the remaining fourteen were rejected.[1] Incidently, the history of revelations would suggest that even those approved have traveled bumpy roads. Parenthetically, it may be helpful to note that when a revelation receives wide notoriety, there is likely to be a spate of reports of other visions. No less than two hundred apparitions were reported in the vicinity of Lourdes

[1] *New Catholic Encyclopedia* (New York: McGraw Hill, 1967), 446.

after the experience of Bernadette. None of these was ever taken seriously.[2]

Usually the disapproval of the local bishop is enough to move a reported revelation out of the doubtful category and into a class of disapproved alleged revelations or, if you will, the false revelations. The case of Saint Joan of Arc shows that sometimes these decisions are reversed. Joan died condemned as a witch by the church court in a decision approved by the University of Paris and was exonerated twenty years later and eventually canonized. Although the process of canonization does not consider the question of the authenticity of visions and revelations, Joan's acceptance as a saint certainly dismisses the charge that her visions were satanic and evil. One gets some real credibility from canonization, although as we have seen, a saint may be wrong about a vision.

There is much dispute about the experience of the young people at Medjugorje. The bishop of the diocese has forcefully and repeatedly called these alleged apparitions false. However, his judgment has been called into question by such theologians as René Laurentin and by at least one archbishop (the retired metropolitan of the ecclesiastical province in which these things occurred). One can certainly make a case for saying that the reported revelations are still in the questionable category.[3]

In the sense that we are using the word, all private revelations begin by being questionable. Those that are not approved or declared false or fraudulent

[2] Sandra Zimdars-Swartz, *Encountering Mary* (Princeton, N.J.: Princeton University Press), 59ff.

[3] René Laurentin, *The Apparitions of Medjugorje Prolonged* (Milford, Oh.: Riehle Foundation, 1987).

remain questionable. Questions may arise because the content of the revelations is esoteric or trite, or because of the personalities of those involved.

Questions may also arise about a reported revelation from several other sources. Suppose for a moment that a person has indeed received an extraordinary grace and feels required to share it with others. Everyone including those favored with the revelation are subject to the vicissitudes of the human mind. Suppose this person became confused during the rigors of interrogation that are usually associated with these things. Suppose in the course of these interrogations the person contradicts himself. Usually these seers are very unsophisticated and often children. When one recalls the interrogations of Bernadette, one wonders that she did not become confused. In fact Joan of Arc did become confused and actually at times was inconsistent in the face of harassment and what we would call brainwashing.[4] Had it not been for her immense notoriety and her epic accomplishments, there is little doubt that Joan's voices would simply have been forgotten as a questionable revelation or even, as her enemies claimed, a false revelation. There is no doubt in my mind that through a special action of divine grace many people have had genuine mystical experiences that have been put permanently in the doubtful file because the testimony has been muddled either by themselves or by others involved.

For those interested, both Poulain and Zimdars-Swartz give many examples of questionable and unauthentic revelations.

[4] S. Stople, *The Maid of Orleans* (New York: Pantheon, 1956), chapters 10, 12.

False Revelations

I have chosen to use the term false revelation, as distinct from a fake or fraud, for a case where the person who experienced the phenomenon is subjectively convinced of its divine origin. In this case both the recipients and the supporters are mistaken, but they are all in good faith. The possible causes of false revelations are many. Severe mental illness, especially a certain kind of paranoid schizophrenia, may create in a subject's mind not only a grandiose need to make some monumental contribution to history but also hallucinatory experiences of a pseudo-mystical type. Once convinced of their divine call, these unbalanced persons may feel justified in fabricating evidence and imagining extraordinary spiritual experiences. This self-importance may even make them feel justified in misleading others. Because of their subjective sincerity they tend to be very convincing. Subjectively they are not lying, so they don't experience guilt. Though deluded, they are essentially not frauds. Frequently the greatest victims of their deceptions are themselves. Within the Church and outside the Church, and especially in the contemporary world of TV preachers, one finds this kind of unbalanced person whose needs for notoriety and power, combined with a charismatic personality, are capable of gaining great attention and support. It is important to differentiate them from religious charlatans and outright frauds. Unlike the frauds, these people sincerely believe that they have a special election by God. False revelations may also arise from a very devout view of life, combined with a suggestive type of personality, clinically called borderline histrionic. Finally, false revelation may occur in a fairly well-balanced person who encounters some of the more untypical functions of the human mind. We will examine such a case shortly, in the book called *A Course in Miracles* (cf. chapter VII and Addendum).

Extremely devout and intelligent people have been misled by false revelations in the past. Church history gives several examples. The very gifted and well-intentioned archbishop of Cambrai, François de Fénelon, was deeply influenced by Madame Guyon.[5] This charismatic lady had an unusual career and is considered one of the founders of the heresy of quietism. This error, which can lead to a complete rejection of one's responsibility for actively following the teachings of the gospel, has often had a strange appeal for devout Christians. In fact, the founder of quietism, Miguel de Molinos, was at one time, spiritual guide of two secretaries of Pope Innocent XI, who eventually presided over the condemnation of his teachings.

Fénelon fell under the influence of Madame Guyon and actually composed some elegant spiritual writings, some of which are tainted with quietism. Guided by her revelations, Madame Guyon and Fénelon founded a group, the Michelins, who were going to reform the world and establish a ring of true prayer, an elite "petite Église". Based on her revelations, the archbishop expected to be the guide of a child (the duke of Burgundy), who was supposed to bring the early triumph of the Michelins. But the prince unfortunately died, and as Poulain observes,

[5] Cf. A. Poulain, *Graces of Interior Prayer* (London: Routledge and Kegan Paul, 1950), 384ff. for an account of this fantastic but informative case. A more detailed account is given by Ronald Knox in *Enthusiasm* (Oxford: Oxford University Press, 1950).

"This talented man spent a great part of his activity in what was pure loss."[6] The works of Madame Guyon and Fénelon are still available in the United States and are published by an evangelical press.[7] Fénelon's writings manifest a real spiritual sense and often considerable literary ability, but he had unfortunately followed a visionary who has been characterized as "half a saint and half a lunatic". We shall later discuss how a sincere but suggestive person may become the innocent source of a false revelation.

Fraudulent Revelations

That frauds abound in any area of human endeavor is news to no discerning person. Religious frauds are interesting primarily because of their ability to deceive large numbers of people who are subjectively disposed to believe in them. Frauds have a long history in Christianity, beginning with Simon Magus in the Acts of the Apostles (8:9). These people knowingly fabricate revelations and exploit paranormal phenomena. As the incredible story of Rasputin indicates, they can do incalculable harm when they have influence over people in authority.[8] They can be individuals of apparent piety. The Franciscan nun Magdalena of the Cross was three times abbess of her monastery at the beginning of the sixteenth century.[9] Complete with self-inflicted stigmata and the ability

[6] Poulain, *Graces of Interior Prayer,* 387.

[7] Bethany House Publisher, Minneapolis, Minn. 55438.

[8] Cf. Robert Massie, *Nicholas and Alexandra* (New York: Dell, 1967), 199–204.

[9] Poulain, *Graces of Interior Prayer,* 340ff.

to levitate above the earth, with ecstasies and a gift of prophecy, she even convinced others that she lived without food. She enjoyed a reputation for extraordinary holiness for several decades. Bishops, clergy, great nobles, and even inquisitors flocked to her. She succeeded in deluding a large number of Spanish theologians who prided themselves on not being easily taken in. However, in danger of death, she confessed that the whole thing was a fabrication and that in fact she inflicted the stigmata on herself. By her own admission she had sold her soul to Satan in return for all of these deceptive gifts, and she actually had to be subjected to exorcism. The fantastic career of this woman alone ought to be a sufficient warning to the gullible.

About a quarter of a century ago a man in Ireland was the subject of a great deal of interest. Whenever he entered a church, the crucifix and occasionally one of the statues would bleed real blood. Medical tests proved that this was real blood mixed with saliva. He eventually confessed that he had practiced for a long time the art of accurate spitting. He would bite the vein under his lips and actually spit at the statue while all were looking at it. Having lost his position as a pseudo-mystic, it is reported that he had a second career as a freelance evangelist in America.

Believers, and especially Christian believers, are taught to think the best of others and not to judge. It makes us vulnerable to deceivers, especially those who use direct conscious deception. If nothing else, this realization should make it a bit more understandable when ecclesiastical authorities are slow and cautious about embracing a claim of private revelation. It is worth noting that a particular source of gullibility and naïveté is the genuine religious belief and fervor that may surround a fraudulent occurrence.[10] There may be a good deal of genuine piety surrounding a fraudulent revelation, but none of it comes from the charlatan himself. It might be useful in this regard to quote here "the devil himself", Joseph Goebbels, surely one of the most sinister figures in modern history. The Nazi propagandist is said to have observed that if you tell a small lie, few will believe it, but if you tell a big lie, many will believe it.

[10] Zimdars-Swartz gives an excellent description of the relationship of people's need to believe in a private revelation and its acceptance in chapters 1 and 2 of *Encountering Mary*.

Six

SOURCES OF ERROR IN PRIVATE REVELATIONS

With these distinctions in mind we are now prepared to consider revelations which are legitimately considered authentic and those which are questionable but for that very reason may someday be considered authentic. We will conclude this part of our discussion with a description of false revelations. Because the alleged recipients were in good faith, this will be done with considerable compassion. Having given the cautions above, nothing further needs to be said about fraudulent revelations.

Rule 4. *A person who is the recipient of an authentic revelation, even a canonized saint, may indeed make errors in understanding that revelation or in reporting experiences which are not authentic revelations.*

We have alluded to this important fact in our second principle above that only human faith (opinion) can be given to a revelation. We have seen that all private revelations come through the prism of the recipient's personality and experiences. No matter how objective their origin in the mercy of divine grace, no matter how unexpected and unsolicited, revelations are all more or less defined within the subjectivity of the individual.

A good example is Saint Bernadette, who sought and expected nothing on that particular February 11, 1858, when she went to gather wood by the River Gave. As distinct and ego-alien as this experience was, she still heard the apparition speak in her own native dialect and she still compared the lady to the appearance of "holy virgins" she had seen. One can with care draw a parallel with the reported response of Saint Peter at the Transfiguration. In an eminently succinct description of a mystical event the apostle is completely overcome by the objective experience, his subjectivity revives a bit, and he suggests building booths, as the Jewish people do on Sukkoth, for Christ and the apparition of the two prophets (Mt 17:1–8).

It is this very subjective element that opens the door to misunderstanding and even error. Saint John of the Cross was aware of the likelihood of error and self-deception, especially in the case of locutions or words heard within the mind but believed to come from God or from some other heavenly being. As we shall see, he believes that often such words are completely the products of the individual's own unconscious mind. He also recognizes that they may be the product of special grace but even then go through the distortion of the individual's subjectivity. He also strongly suggests that the locutions may be the work of Satan.[1]

[1] St. John of the Cross, *The Ascent of Mt. Carmel,* trans. K. Kavanaugh and O. Rodriguez (Washington, D.C.: Institute of Carmelite Studies, 1973), book III, 11–15, 229–37.

Poulain gives five general reasons why authentic revelations may contain errors; (a) faulty interpretation on the part of the recipient or others; (b) a tendency to use a revelation to write history rather than to use it symbolically; (c) the tendency of the visionary to mix subjective expectations and preconceived ideas with the action of divine grace; (d) a subsequent altering or amplification of the testimony after the revelation; and (e) errors made in good faith by those who record the testimony. Anyone actively interested in private revelation would do well to memorize this list, which we will now discuss in detail.

A. Faulty Interpretation of the Revelation

One must recall that most revelations are internal locutions or words (either clearly heard as if pronounced, or concepts that one thinks of without putting them into words). They are not actually auditory, since there is no operation of the process of hearing. They may be inner visions, either appearing to be in the external world (Bernadette saw the Lady; the spectators saw nothing), or they are in the imaging faculty of the mind, as Saint Teresa describes her visions. Many times revelations are both words experienced in the mind, and quasi-visual experiences, that is, occurring without any operation of the organic mechanism for hearing and sight. In such cases, the individual does not have the clues for assuring objectivity that one has when experiencing ordinary physical hearing or sight. The recipient is like a person adrift in the sea on a very foggy day. One has no points of reference and does not know where the sky begins and the sea ends. In such a situation one's preconceived ideas, hopes, and expectations may easily cloud the understanding of the revelation. The powerful painting of Saint Joan of Arc by Jules Bastien-Lepage (1848–1884) hanging in the foyer of the New York Metropolitan Museum of Art illustrates the confusing quality of private revelation in a graphic way. The realism of Joan's figure and environment contrast sharply with the visionary outlines of saints, but still the viewer is left with the impression that the visions are as real as any of the details of physical environment.

A sad example of misunderstanding of a revelation is to be found in the case of Saint Joan. Because she was so carefully interrogated, we have accurate accounts of her testimony. "I inquired of my voices whether I should be burned; they answered me that I should trust in Our Lord and that He would aid me . . . St. Catherine told me that I would receive succour".[2]

She understandably thought that these words of the vision which had guided her so faithfully in life indicated her deliverance. She added: "As a rule the voices tell me that I shall be delivered by a great victory and afterwards they say; fear not because of thy martyrdom. It will bring thee at last to paradise."[3]

Unfortunately, Joan explained that she thought the word martyrdom meant "the great pains and adversity that (she) suffered in prison". She actually thought that she would be delivered before the hour of death.[4] Perhaps this poignant misunderstanding, a

[2] A. Poulain, *Graces of Interior Prayer* (London: Routledge and Kegan Paul, 1950), 324.

[3] Ibid.

[4] Ibid., 324.

mistake as it were, contains one of the most powerful spiritual messages in the life of one whom Winston Churchill calls "the purest figure in European history for a thousand years".[5] This is an oft-repeated experience. Every spiritual director has heard it many times: a devout soul is so sure that a certain course of action is God's will, but it does not work out as expected. This disappointment becomes a real test of faith. In the case of Joan, "the great victory" was given after her death. In fact, it was won by the death she did not expect, but accepted. History would go beyond her mistaken interpretation. Her great victory is celebrated by writers as diverse as Mark Twain, George Bernard Shaw, and the prime minister of the country she defeated. Those interested in private revelations would do well to ponder this strange fact: Joan understood enough to change the history of Europe, but she did not understand her own destiny. Yet, there is another side. Many a private revelation or inspiration has saved a life. The following account was given to me by Brother Brendan Lague, O. F. M., who had been a missionary in China when the Japanese army invaded the country. Up to the time of my interview with Brother Brendan, when he was in his seventies, no other event of any mysterious nature ever happened to him. Apparently he never reported any after this interview. He sat in his little informal art studio and gave the following account of a totally unexpected event that saved his life.

[5] Winston Churchill, *History of the English Speaking Peoples* vol 1, (London: Dodd, Mead, 1956), 306–9. His entire assessment of Joan of Arc can be read with profit.

Brother Brendan recounted how on May 14, 1943, the Japanese army entered the walled city of Shasi, province of Hupeh, from one direction while the friars escaped through the gate on the opposite side of the city. Escape was necessary because they had been told that the army would kill all foreigners they found. Brother was quite young, but he lagged behind taking care of an elderly friar. When they arrived at the top of an adjoining hill and saw the path divide, they did not know which way their confreres had gone. They were preparing to go to the right when a figure of a man was suddenly in front of them. He said, "No, go to the left." Brother Brendan said to himself, "It is Saint Joseph." He was clothed simply in ordinary Chinese attire but was not oriental. Brother Brendan could not remember whether he heard the man speak in English or Chinese, but for the moment he was quite certain that this non-Oriental person standing there in the midst of the Chinese countryside was Saint Joseph. They followed his instructions, and as they ran down the path to the left, they could hear machine gun fire right behind them toward the path to the right. Had they gone to the right they would have been killed immediately. I have it on the word of his contemporaries that Brother Brendan was a person of very sound mind. He had no unusual personality traits, nor, as I mentioned, did he report any other remarkable experiences. I was not able to interview him immediately before his death, but I assume in the absence of any reports that nothing else like this ever took place again. This is an example of a completely unexpected experience out of the blue, as it were, which saved a person's life. It needs no interpretation. Unlike Joan of Arc, he had no opportunity to interpret the experience subjectively except for the one single detail of the identity of the person. Without any other information he was convinced that he had seen Saint Joseph. In this case, he did not misinterpret the message of the vision. It saved his life.

Promises Made by Visions

It is important to add a note here on promises which reportedly have been made by visions. Various private revelations contain promises of salvation for those who follow the instruction of the vision. The most popular of these are the promise made to those who wear the scapular and the promise to those who observe the first Friday in honor of the Sacred Heart. Those who faithfully fulfill these promises are assured of salvation. These promises can never be understood outside the general context of Scripture and sacred Tradition. It is generally recognized by the devout that those who observe these promises must also observe the gospel and the teaching of the Church. Pope Benedict XIV spoke directly to this question when he commented on the reported promise of Our Lady of Mount Carmel to Saint Simon Stock.[6] "She did not say that those who have worn the scapular will be saved from eternal fire by this means alone, without having done anything else. Good works and perseverance and well doing are necessary to eternal salvation."

Pope Benedict XIV also points out that certain statements of Our Lord in the gospel promising salvation for the fulfillment of certain conditions

[6] Poulain, *Graces of Interior Prayer,* 327.

must always be understood in the general context of the Scriptures themselves. For example, fulfilling the command of Our Lord about almsgiving and eating his flesh in Holy Communion do not suffice by themselves to bring salvation. Although they may appear to be stated that way, it is obvious that these two promises made by the Lord himself must be seen in the general context of all of his teaching.[7]

B. A Need to Rewrite Biblical History and Give Prophecy

Another source of error is to use a private revelation to rewrite history and to fail to recognize that these revelations are symbolic. It often happens to a person who will experience a very highly articulated inner vision of biblical scenes or perhaps what is assumed to be a future event. Not understanding the subjective element in such an experience, even a saint may arrive at the unwarranted conclusion that the experience represents historical reality or the future event as it is to be. One needs to mention here a genre of mystical literature that is still very popular. Such mystics as Saint Bridget, Saint Frances of Rome, Blessed Veronica of Binasco, María of Ágreda, and Anna Katharina Emmerich all recorded long and even complete visions of the events of the gospel especially as experienced by the Blessed Virgin Mary.

Presently wide attention is given to a similar book called *The Poem of the Man-God* by Maria Valtorta.[8]

[7] Ibid., 327.

[8] Maria Valtorta, *The Poem of the Man-God* (Isola dell' Liri, Italy: Centro Ed. Valtortiana, 1986).

Some sobering facts culled by Poulain need to be recalled when we consider this book. In a document of considerable intellectual insight Maria Angillara, who succeeded Saint Frances of Rome as superior of the Congregation of Oblates, writes:

> Many of the things that she saw when she was in ecstasy must be considered as being merely pious meditations and contemplations due to her own action especially those that concern Our Savior's life and passion; this is easily apparent in reading them. We cannot, however, deny true revelations may be mingled with them, leaving the task of discrimination to the pious reader and to superiors I will without distinction transcribe all that the ancient manuscript contains.[9]

Poulain took the trouble to compare biblical dates given by various seers and writers and finds great discrepancy. For instance, reports of the time of the death of the Blessed Virgin Mary vary immensely. Saint Bridget reports that it was fourteen years after the death of Christ. María of Ágreda, twenty-one years, and Anna Katharina Emmerich thirteen years. A most fascinating lady we will come to, Saint Elizabeth of Schoenau, reported a year and a half. They can't all be right! Anna Katharina Emmerich perhaps summed it all up very well in her critique of María of Ágreda when she said that this Spanish visionary had taken her visions too literally and should have understood them allegorically and spiritually.

The writings of Maria Valtorta, composed in this century and now receiving considerable popular

---

[9] Poulain, *Graces of Interior Prayer,* 329.

interest, must be seen in light of all of this information. [10] *The Poem of the Man-God* demonstrates a mind of keen intelligence and genuine literary skill, as well as deep religious devotion. Unfortunately the publishers of the *Poem of the Man-God* create the false impression that it has papal approval. In fact, the opposite is true. [11] Those who find these books helpful for their own devotion should bear in mind that this is not a fifth gospel, any more than the revelations of María of Ágreda or Emmerich. In the use of the *Poem of the Man-God* it is also important to

[10] Actually the *Poem of the Man-God* was placed on the Index of Forbidden Books by Pope John XXIII on January 5, 1960. When the ten-volume edition of the *Poem* was projected by the publishers (Pisani) in 1961, the *Osservatore Romano,* the official Vatican newspaper, commented (Dec. 1, 1961) that this work "has no scientific value, includes the same material contained in the four volumes already condemned by the Holy Office, on December 16, 1959 (A.A.S., vol lii, p.60) and therefore must retain the same condemnation according to Canon 1399." Although the Index had been abrogated Cardinal Joseph Ratzinger, writing of the poem in a letter to Cardinal Siri, archbishop of Genoa, on January 31, 1985, said the following:

"A decision against distributing and recommending a work which had not been lightly condemned may be reversed but only after profound changes that neutralize the harm which such publication could bring forth among the ordinary faithful."

"[*The Poem of the Man-God* has already been] examined scientifically and placed in a well known category of mental sickness. . . . The facts added to the second edition do not change the nature of the work, which evidences being a mountain of childishness, of fantasies and of historical and exegetical falsehoods, diluted in a subtly sensual atmosphere, through the presence of a group of women in the company of Jesus. On the whole it is a heap of pseudo-religiosity. Therefore, also for the second edition the judgment of the Church to condemn it retains its validity."

[11] Valtorta, *Poem,* insert in vol 1 signed by E. Pisani.

recall that Maria Valtorta is described in the preface as having spent the last decade of her life in a state similar to catatonic schizophrenia. [12]

These very compromising facts, including the strongest ecclesiastical disapproval after her death, do not negate the possibility that she was a genuinely devout Christian and loyal member of the Church. This case alone should give caution to devout readers not to build their spiritual lives or form their personal world vision on this book or, for that matter, on any other book of alleged private revelation. We were given the Sacred Scriptures as the foundation of our spiritual lives.

C. Subjective Need

The third common source of error in private revelation is one that we have already alluded to, that is, the comingling of the subjective needs of the individual with the action of divine grace. For instance, a strong inspiration prayerfully received may appear to the individual to continue over a period beyond the time when it has actually ended. Or persons may assume that they are inspired in what they say and do, and yet the recipients are now experiencing only their own memories as a kind of aftershock.

Preconceived ideas may also weigh heavily on the individual's perception of a private revelation. It is reported that Saint Catherine of Siena learned from a vision of the Blessed Virgin Mary herself that the Immaculate Conception was not true. Actually at this time the Dominicans and Franciscans were locked in

[12] Ibid.

theological controversy over this question. It seemed to the saint that Our Lady took the side of the Dominicans.[13]

Saint Colette, the foundress of a reform of the Poor Clares brought preconceived ideas into her visions in a way that is really not surprising.[14] She apparently heard the legend that Saint Anne had married three times and had several daughters. Saint Colette saw the whole family in a vision. Obviously the line of reality is hard or even impossible to draw in such a case. We have no scriptural knowledge of the family of Saint Anne or even of her name. Where do preconceived ideas end and revelations begin?

The subjective may at times be a rich source of strength and accomplishment in the case of an individual who is sincerely responsive to a providential call. For the infinite to communicate with the finite, the limited thoughts and images of the human mind must be utilized. Images of all three of Joan's favorite saints were in the parish church at Domremy. Saint Margaret of Antioch and Saint Catherine of Alexandria were subjects of legends about the great bravery of young women. Saint Michael was patron of the house of Valois, to which the Dauphin belonged. Stople seems to pose the intelligent question: Did not the infinity of God use these finite images to communicate with Joan? Did she not claim that the Divine Being himself sent her on her impossible errand? And does not objective history indicate that what Joan said her voices promised was, in fact, fulfilled?

[13] Poulain quotes Pope Benedict XIV. Some have blamed this opinion of Catherine on an error by her biographers. Cf. *Graces of Interior Prayer*, 338.
[14] Ibid.

Stople opens the mind of the reader to the mysterious complexities of a genuine revelation and its subjective elements.[15] In a complex situation like the call of Joan of Arc, including variables completely beyond human understanding, it is not surprising that subjective elements may easily enter in and even be very productive.

Another opening for the subjective needs of the seer occurs when the visionary is also a person of unusual natural talent. At times the scope of extended natural talent goes beyond any present scientific explanation, adding to the mystery. We do not have this problem, for instance, with Bernadette or Catherine Labouré or the children of Fatima. They have always been seen as persons of somewhat average abilities. However, suppose a vision is experienced by a child prodigy or a genius. Present-day psychology has as yet no real understanding of the child prodigy—for instance, someone like Yehudi Menuhin, who was a world-class violinist at the age of seven, or Schubert, who composed sophisticated classical music as a child. Psychology has no adequate explanation of these abilities. Suppose such talents are joined to a life that abounds in mystical graces. This appears to be the case of Saint Hildegard, whom we have mentioned. She had a knowledge of Latin and music, even though she had never studied either. Without any knowledge of Latin she grasped the meaning of an entire passage and yet could not define the words or give any of the tenses. She claimed that she derived the knowledge from a divine light that she had had from the age of three. It is quite possible

[15] S. Stople, *The Maid of Orleans* (New York: Pantheon, 1956), 57–61.

that here we are dealing with both a child prodigy and a great mystic. This complicates the situation. Along with her mystical writings of considerable beauty and occasional theological ambiguity, she wrote a book on physics and medicine that is completely fanciful and filled with ideas which were popular when science was insufficiently separated from alchemy. To quote Poulain, "She seemed to have had exceptional graces and great illusions."[16] Were this remarkable woman alive, experts on psychology of learning and the study of mysticism might be able to work together to filter out her natural gifts from her supernatural ones.

I have been tempted to omit the case of Saint Elizabeth of Schoenau, a friend of Saint Hildegard. This saintly soul was a Benedictine abbess, who had spiritual gifts that got her into serious trouble. It is only to warn my own contemporaries who think that saints can't be wrong that I summarize this case from Poulain's description. When the relics of Saint Ursula and her companions were discovered, in 1156, Saint Elizabeth interviewed the departed souls to whom these relics belonged, with the assistance of her guardian angel. Foolishly her directors encouraged her in this enterprise, and she persevered in praying the deceased back to these interviews even when the visions appeared to have come to an end. She was convinced that God was the author of her revelations. These biographies of the deceased are filled with historical inaccuracies and impossibilities. This case especially points out the danger of seeking more and

---

[16] Poulain, *Graces of Interior Prayer,* 333.

more information from a revelation and the danger of using a visionary for such information.[17]

This strange tale of a person who was in fact a saint should be a warning to those who encourage the continuation of visions and try to use these as a source of everyday information or in theological controversy. This is, I think, an abuse of a visionary as a person and will lead inevitably to disaster. Visionaries themselves will probably be unaware of their own subjectivity and may in fact "keep their visions going" in response to the needs of others.

In the case of prolonged revelations, like those of Saint Elizabeth of Schoenau, I would suggest that if these communications continue and are recorded, the transcripts should be stored in completely confidential files and especially that the visionaries not be given questions to ask the apparition. Since even saints get confused in this kind of situation, how unfair it is to young people—who may be operating in total innocence and with no ability for self-criticism—to be asked to continue to give daily reports, as is frequently done. I agree with Poulain that such activity is filled with dangers and may lead to discrediting what initially may have been a genuine private revelation.

I also think that it is equally unwise to allow devout souls to place devotional articles near where an apparition is said to be taking place, leading to the unwarranted conclusion that Our Lady or some saint "blessed" these objects. In extremely rare events an object is believed to have been left behind by a vision. The most famous example is the mysterious tilma or

[17] Ibid., 332.

cloak of Juan Diego bearing the image of the Virgin of Guadalupe. Such a remarkable object is very different from a rosary left on a table in a room where an individual in a trancelike state is having an interior experience of a heavenly presence. It also might be observed that the practice of blessing rosaries has always been reserved to the clergy, and the Church has never suggested that the Blessed Mother is a priest. Probably little or no harm is done to the naïve who become involved in this kind of behavior, but there is a very real danger that a genuine private revelation will be discredited and ignored by those who should heed its message because of what too easily falls into the category of superstition.

D. Errors from Remembering and Recording

Once the mysterious operation of a genuine revelation comes to a conclusion, the recipient's ideas and theories about it are subject to the same vagaries of recollection and reporting that surround any kind of human knowledge. The recipient of a revelation can forget things, have difficulty putting it all into words, and even select the wrong words to describe what has happened. This is especially true if the individual has had an experience of life beyond the grave, either of the heavenly realm of saints (which eye has not seen), or the unthinkably terrible destiny of the damned, or even the experience of Purgatory. There are no words accurately to record such things. One of the most telling examples may be the very obviously symbolic visions (much more intellectual than imaginative) of the purification of the just given by Saint Catherine of Genoa.

As for paradise, God has placed no doors there.
Whoever wishes to enter, does so.
All-merciful God stands there with His arms open,
waiting to receive us into His glory.
I also see, however,
that the divine essence is so pure and light-filled
—much more than we can imagine—
that the soul that has but the slightest imperfection
would rather throw itself into a thousand hells
than appear thus before the divine presence.
Tongue cannot express nor heart understand
the full meaning of purgatory,
which the soul willingly accepts as a mercy,
the realization that that suffering is of no importance
compared to the removal of the impediment of sin.[18]

No one familiar with the text can doubt that she is describing a reality grasped by the mind rather than by some imaginative scene when she says these things.[19]

The visions of Saint Catherine of Siena and Saint Teresa are also intellectual visions like this one of Saint Catherine of Genoa.[20] Frequently the mystical writers seem to be using these images as parables. At least in the case of Saint Catherine of Genoa I am convinced that this was partially done for pedagogical reasons.

Another source of confusion is the problem of recalling something that is an internal experience. Readers may be familiar with this problem when they have tried to recall a dream (also an internal

[18] S. Hughes and B. Groeschel, *Catherine of Genoa* (New York: Paulist Press, 1979), 78.
[19] Ibid.
[20] Cf. Poulain, *Graces of Interior Prayer,* 300–306 for a thorough review of the topic.

event) after a period of time. Similar problems confront the visionary or recipient of a revelation. This has led to visionaries revealing details decades later which were never alluded to in their original testimony. Wise spiritual directors should counsel a visionary against expanding testimony later on. It is one of the great qualities of Bernadette's testimony that she never added a single detail and resisted all attempts of writers and artists to amplify or crystalize her experience. The only image that Bernadette ever said reminded her of what she had seen was a plain little Madonna which had been placed in the washhouse of the convent where she went to live as a Sister of Charity. This image was apparently made before the events of Lourdes and bore no direct relationship to Bernadette's original report. It is significant that she rejected all artistic representations of what she had reported and all attempts to add to her testimony.

Perhaps it is an error in memory that is the source of reports that the Blessed Virgin instructed the children of Fatima to pray for the souls in hell. This would be a theological impossibility.[21] If this report is accurate, then the problem of memory may explain the visionaries' error. If it is not true, then we come to the last source of error in our discussion.

E. Errors in Reporting

Those who report or record private revelations also may inadvertently make corrections, amplifications,

---

[21] Francis Johnston, *Fatima, The Great Sign* (Rockford, Ill.: Tan Books, 1980), 33. In fact the reports of this vision are ambiguous.

and minor additions. When the experiences of visionaries become known, a general atmosphere of great excitement surrounds them. Until recently, this super-charged atmosphere was unfortunately and inaccurately called hysteria. A better contemporary term might be media hype. Anyone visiting the scene of such reports—be they in the past, like Lourdes and Fatima, or in the present, like Medjugorje—feels the electricity in the air. Those attempting to make an accurate report are subject to the same feelings of excitement. Sometimes even skeptics are completely swept up in this atmosphere and may return as devout supporters of the revelation. Even the objective reporter, like Wayne Weible, may become involved in distortion.[22] This is particularly true if the recorder of such events is a pious dabbler who has a message to give the world and would like to put it, as it were, on a flyer attached to the private revelation.

Finally, there is the case of open falsification done for pious motives. The editors of the works of Saint Catherine of Siena have been accused of changing her testimony on the denial of the Immaculate Conception. In the archives of the Dominican order there is

[22] Zimdars-Swartz cites the reports of Wayne Weible, a reporter who has become a fervent supporter of Medjugorje while remaining a Protestant. Weible's interpretation of a parchment-like object, purported to have been given to one of the seers by Our Lady, is contradicted by René Laurentin, a priest theologian who also supports the authenticity of these revelations. Both of these men enthusiastically accept the general testimony of the seers, but obviously disagree on the interpretation of this object which Laurentin sees as having more in common with magic. Cf. Zimdars-Swartz, *Encountering Mary* (Princeton, N.J.: Princeton University Press, 1991), 236, and René Laurentin, *The Apparitions of Medjugorje Prolonged* (Milford, Oh.: Riehle Foundation, 1987).

a manuscript dating from 1398 that contains the account of this ecstasy which occurred in 1377.[23] Pope Benedict XIV, examining all the materials relating to this apparent mistake in Saint Catherine's apparitions, at least suggests the possibility that she may have been deceived by her own preconceived ideas. Who knows?

The various books of private revelations giving the details of biblical scenes which we have mentioned previously are most frequently the objects of editing. Poulain gives the example of a change made by editors in the German edition of Anna Katharina Emmerich's works. Her original statement that Saint James was present at the death of the Virgin Mary was simply taken out in the later editions because it failed to agree with the chronology of the Acts of the Apostles. Poulain calls such activities deplorable and suggests that the publishers may have been motivated by the desire to sell books. He also states that such editing went on in the writings of María of Ágreda whereby objectionable parts were deleted and suppressed. This kind of activity prevents the reader from critically evaluating the original testimony and is a serious literary deception.

A related source of error comes from the biographers who record the lives of visionaries and others of saintly reputation. The discerning reader should be able to tell in a few pages if the biographer is attempting a factual account of well-documented events, some of which may be extraordinary, or is presenting in a completely uncritical way every story he can lay his hands on. A case in point is the remarkable life of the Capuchin Padre Pio of Pietrel-

---

[23] Poulain, *Graces of Interior Prayer,* 339.

cina. The life of this saintly friar abounded in paranormal phenomena of the most inexplicable type. I have spoken to two people to whom Padre Pio had personally revealed their sins and failings in a helpful way. Unfortunately, a person with such gifts attracts many histrionic people and is surrounded by what we would call media hype. The ordinary parameters of credibility are easily broken by paranormal gifts, opening unbounded vistas of imaginary claims and fables for those who like this sort of thing. In 1951 Father Clement Neubauer, the minister general of the Capuchin order, described to me a very popular biography of Padre Pio, written by two clergymen, as filled with inaccuracies and unsubstantiated tales. Separating fact from fiction became a real challenge for more serious biographers who sought to serve the truth while presenting a positive picture of the saintly padre.[24]

[24] Among authors who have sought to gather the facts honestly see C. Bernard Ruffin, *Padre Pio: The True Story,* 2nd ed. (Huntington, Ind.: OSV Press, 1991) and John Schug, O.F.M. Cap., *A Padre Pio Profile* (Petersham, Mass.: St. Bede Press, 1987).

Seven

FALSE REVELATIONS—
A SYMPATHETIC VIEW

We have defined false revelations, as distinct from
frauds, as those experiences which a sincere person
honestly believes come from God and which he believes reflect the special operation of divine grace. Let
it be said at the outset that it is almost as difficult to
be certain that all aspects of such an experience are
false as it is to be certain that all parts of authentic
experience are truly from a divine origin. How can
one ever know that a sincere but deluded soul is in no
way responding to a special grace given, since by its
very theological definition, grace is always in reality
a free relationship of God to an individual? The idea
of grace-in-general is as theoretical and abstract as the
idea of sin-in-general. Both sin and grace exist in
individuals. Consequently, persons deluded by their
own minds into thinking that God has selected them
for some special gift of knowledge may still lead a
very virtuous life. We have seen this already in the
case of Saint Elizabeth of Schoenau and her talking
relics. The conclusion is that even a heroically virtuous person may respond to grace in a way that is
strongly affected by subjective expectations and
needs. This may cause them unconsciously and in-
culpably to alter and even fabricate a profound religious experience to fit their expectations.

Some Sources of False Revelation

False revelation may arise from any one of the subjective reasons we have given above affecting the accurate reporting of authentic revelations and from some other sources. The uncertainty of the historical times or of life situations may cause an insecurity which leads people not only to a virtuous and healthy dependence on God but also to a mistaken belief that God is leading them by extraordinary signs. Our Lord himself warned against this when he said that those who sought signs would receive no encouraging sign but that of Jonah, that is, no encouraging sign at all (Mt 12:39). (I have always believed that this passage made the most sense when it was read with an ironic Jewish sense of humor.) In difficult times which one of us has not prayed for a special providential sign, although we might not have called it a private revelation? In fact, what we were looking for was a private revelation in very modest proportions.

When the pillars of one's certitude begin to rock, the believer is all the more likely to look for new supports directly from God. Christ also warns against this, indicating that times were coming when people would claim that the Messiah was here or there or out in the desert (Mt 24:26).

At present, when there is obviously a great deal of theological confusion and some real uncertainty in various quarters of what was once called the Catholic world, many would like to hear a direct response from someone who could give a word of assurance from above. I personally believe that such assurances can be and are given through private revelations. Unfortunately, this very same need can spawn innumerable inauthentic signs, wonders, seers, and odd phenomena like moving statues and weeping pictures. I take the point of view that each phenomenon which has some credibility about it must be objectively evaluated by the norms of common sense, and even by scientific inquiry if that is pertinent. There are, unfortunately, no great crowds to gather around to support the idea of rational inquiry. Two typical responses are unbounded credulity on the one hand, and a timid rejection on the other. This rejection carries with it the hope that if there is in fact a mysterious force at work, it will soon go away. This response may mask a real skepticism that anything supernatural could ever happen.

Another source of false revelation is the profound need to find God, the source of their being and their destiny. This elemental dynamic, the phenomenological source of all religious activity, is usually understated by students of human nature and is taken into account far less frequently than is warranted by the facts of history. The same need that built the pyramids and founded the vast religious movements of the world, for a variety of reasons, apparent or hidden, may be unleashed in an individual's life at a particular time.

The desire to fulfill the need to find God, this most basic spiritual thirst, may give rise to vivid religious experiences that seem to the individual to have their origin completely outside the self. One has only to scan the biographies of the founders of great religions of the world to realize that they were all motivated and in fact engulfed by the same kind of experience that we are calling private revelation. How much or how little did these experiences originate in the loving grace of a personal God, the God of Abraham and the Father of Our Lord Jesus Christ? This is a question never to be adequately answered in this world.

But insofar as a powerful religious experience is purported to be a revelation of God but in fact does not come from him, we must call it false revelation. It may be a very genuine, beautiful, and even fruitful experience, but it is not a revelation in the sense that we are using the word. It does not come directly from the providence of God. It is my contention that, like all kinds of theological misconceptions arrived at innocently, a religious experience that contradicts the teaching of the Church may be a very valid religious experience of personal need and of God's response to that need. However, because of the error of interpretation of the recipient, it is a false revelation from the point of view of our Faith.

Paradoxically, because the person who reports a false revelation may be living in a state of grace (that is, a vital relationship with God), there may be a great deal of borrowed truth in the reported experience. The written account may be far more subtle and spiritual than Saint Elizabeth's interviews with the relics (which were clearly false revelations); yet it is not an authentic revelation, because of the substantial error involved. For this reason I respect the sacred books of Oriental religions, which record the honest strivings of many great souls to find God without the benefit of Sacred Scripture. I have learned wisdom from these books, but for me they are not revelations, although these works, indeed, may have been the fruit of God assisting his children by grace. Because of the lack of a knowledge of the mystery of the Savior either as promised to Israel or fulfilled in Jesus

Christ, the Oriental scriptures must represent the things of God with serious distortions. I recognize that there are now those in Christianity who make little distinction between these Oriental mystical texts and private revelation or even public revelation (Scripture) within the Church. I emphatically disagree. It appears that to fail to make this distinction is in fact tacitly to deny the absolute necessity of the saving grace of Christ and the uniqueness of the Paschal Mystery.

This is even more obvious when we consider our contemporaries who despite having the gospel message easily available to them have preferred their own experiences apart from the reality of grace. I consider these revelations false, not because the writers are necessarily devoid of grace but because their ideas spring from minds unenlightened by the authoritative teaching of Christ. There may be people living side by side with Christians who, because of their own sincere adherence to a non-Christian religion, find the gospel closed to them. I do not refer to these people. I refer rather to those who could know Christ but do not know him, however innocently they may have arrived at this situation. An example may help to illustrate this.

An Example—A Course in Miracles

I recall my utter astonishment, almost a feeling of disorientation, when Helen Schucman and William Thetford, my professors in psychology at the College of Physicians and Surgeons of Columbia University, told me in 1969 of Helen's strange encounter with "the Son of God". Helen was an extremely brilliant Jewish woman, who described herself up to that time (about 60 years of age), as being an agnostic bordering on atheism. There were inconsistencies in this position because she claimed to have prayed the Rosary frequently (and confusedly) since she had accidentally visited Lourdes as a child. She was so impressed by this event and by what seemed to her a spiritual sign (seeing the "shooting stars", or meteorites always visible the eve of Saint Lawrence) that she had obtained baptism from a fundamentalist Christian minister on her return from the shrine.

Sometime before I became her student, she had an experience of light, an imaginative vision, in a subway train. She saw light filling the car and shining from the faces of the people around her. Her husband, the most religious atheist I have ever known (so you never met an unreligious believer?), reassured her at the time by saying that this was a very common mystical experience and if she didn't pay attention to it, it would go away. Sometime after she felt compelled to start writing long pages, which generally scanned into blank verse. These pages grew into a three-volume work, *A Course in Miracles,* and a book of poetry.[1] The books have certain very puzzling characteristics. First of all, they do not represent Helen's own thought or convictions. When I met her, she still didn't know whether she believed in God at all. Years later I would still observe this separation in her thought and her conflict about the book. She would often be angry at the book. She once told me: "I hate that damned book."

[1] Helen Schucman, *A Course in Miracles* (New York: Foundation for Inner Peace, 1975), and *The Gifts of God* (Tiburon, Calif.: Foundation for Inner Peace, 1982).

The books are centered on a "Son of God" who at times seems to be the Christ of orthodox Christianity and sometimes an avatar of an Eastern religion. Since one sentence appears to contradict the one preceding it, I found it impossible to discover any real theological perspective, and I came to regard these writings as a kind of religious poetry. Some passages are very strange, defining as real only what is everlasting—a Hindu frame of thought. Suffering is not real; neither is sin. This is difficult to swallow in New York City. There are beautiful passages on forgiveness, as well as eccentric (at least for the Christian) denials of the spiritual meaning of sacrifice. What do we do with the Cross?

Helen at this time was drawn to the Catholic Church and attended Mass frequently, but did not feel impelled to join formally. Being ethnically Jewish, she told me that she felt that she was part of the Church before "you Gentiles made all these rules". Her devotion to the Blessed Virgin Mary was genuine, as was her devotion to Christ. These devotions it seemed to me were uncompromised by her book. Interestingly enough, when describing the book, she would say that she knew the meaning of the sentence she was writing, but did not know what was coming after it. She did not appear to hear words, but to know what they would be. This phenomenon is called internal dictation and is different from automatic writing, in which the individual does not even know the context. Her experience very much fits what Poulain would call an intellectual locution.[2]

---

[2] A. Poulain, *Graces of Interior Prayer* (London: Routledge and Kegan Paul, 1950), 300.

William Thetford became her scribe. This brilliant man had several mysterious aspects to his life. It was revealed after his retirement from Columbia that for years he had been an agent of the CIA. He claimed to have been at the first fission experiment at the University of Chicago, called the Manhattan Project. One suspects that he may have been a CIA agent even then. He appeared to me to exercise a great control over Helen and to be editing her writings, even though she felt that she could not change a word. Although he was most kind to me, I always felt that he was not entirely capable of the honest, open sharing that is necessary for a friendship. As a result of his experience with Helen, he had become extremely interested in what he called spiritual teaching and phenomena, but in retrospect I don't think he ever actually was a believing Christian. In his defense I must say that he honestly tried to follow the teachings of this Course.

For Helen, the Course had become a burden; for Bill it had become the Bible.

Because of the many allusions in this Course to the "Son of God" and because much of its teaching is parallel to that of the gospel, I tried to open doors of the Church to my two friends—perhaps unwisely. I believed that with what was going on in their lives, they would be helped by a good dose of Christian theology. In retrospect, I believe that this was true of Helen but that Bill remained essentially unrelated to any kind of orthodox Christian teaching. It seems to me now that at that time Helen had faith and that Bill did not. Others became involved, and I regret at this time that some were not prepared. I now wish that I had gone back to read Poulain again since I had only a superficial knowledge of his work at that time.

Against Helen's better judgment, the Course was published first in a small private edition and then in a larger public edition. To her great discomfort Helen's identity became known. She was embarrassed and confided to me her fear that the Course could become a cult. I agreed with her but had no real influence in stopping the publication, which was very much the work of Bill Thetford. Other books appeared, reflecting the various positive and beautiful parts of the Course related to forgiveness and accepting reality, an idea akin either to the traditional teaching on abandonment to Divine Providence or, if one preferred, to the quietism of Fénelon. Unfortunately, *A Course in Miracles* has become something of a sophisticated cult, and its followers are caught up in the general wave of Gnosticism that one observes as genuine religious conviction wanes in our society.

Two very disturbing but insightful facts gradually came into view for me and threw some light on this very strange chapter in my own life. One was the incredible darkness that descended upon Helen Schucman in the last years of her life. This woman who had written so eloquently that suffering really did not exist spent the last two years of her life in the blackest psychotic depression I have ever witnessed. Her husband cared for her with an incredible devotion, and her friends did the best they could. But it was almost frightening to be with her. I clearly observed that the denial of the reality of suffering could have catastrophic consequences.

The second fact that emerged was that Helen's mother had embraced Christian Science and had read the spiritual writings of Mary Baker Eddy to her as a child. A review of Helen's Course and of the writings of Mrs. Eddy would reveal many similarities about the denial of the reality of suffering. There is also the unorthodox representation of Christ, who is by no means denied, but so distorted that the "Son of God" becomes a vague mystical figure who conveniently fits into any doctrinal crevice the individual may carve out for him. One writer, Kenneth Wapnick, has acknowledged in his own writings the doctrinal discrepancies between the Course and any traditional biblical Christianity.[3]

In retrospect, it is my opinion that this Course is a good example of a false revelation. Helen's experiences, I believe, arose from the profound religious need and sensitivity that went all the way back to her visit to Lourdes as a child. As old age and the end of life came into view, her genuine need to make some sense out of the journey of life caused her to bring up from the past the readings of Christian Science and other literature pertaining to spirituality that she had encountered years before. Her husband was a rare books expert and often brought spiritual books home. I believe that Helen's attraction specifically to the Catholic Church went all the way back to her visit to Lourdes, but this attraction was eclipsed by the experience of writing the Course. As her illness became more acute and obviously terminal, her mind could no longer mediate between these conflicting forces. Perhaps the most powerful conflict came not between the Catholicism she admired and the Course, rather it was the conflict between her ex-

[3] Kenneth Wapnick, *Forgiveness and Jesus* (Farmingdale, N.Y.: Coleman Publishing Co., 1966). This work attempts to interpret the Course in orthodox Christian terms, an interpretation he later reversed; see Addendum.

perience of reality, especially her suffering, and the idea of the Course that suffering does not really exist. Her desperate depression, in which at times there were glimpses of hope, was, I believe, an attempt to control and dampen the anger that this conflict generated. I recall imploring the intervention of Our Lady many times to seek divine assistance for this troubled soul who was so devoted to her.

An uncanny detail ends this short account. Helen's husband arranged an orthodox Jewish funeral for her. As I was preparing to offer a Mass for the repose of her soul early that morning before going to the funeral, I opened the missal to discover that it was the Feast of Our Lady of Lourdes, the anniversary of the first apparition to Saint Bernadette.

What can one learn from this strange account? First, that the human mind has dimensions and functions of which we have little knowledge, and hence we need to proceed with caution when we face the unusual or paranormal. Freud, Jung, and many others have written about the unknown depths of human psychological functioning. The power of the unconscious is never to be underestimated. This is also true when it comes to functions related to the spiritual life and especially to things like private revelation. Also, we learn that in religious matters, in questions related to the most intimate life of the soul, one cannot escape from the need to be led by the teachings of the Faith. I came out of my experience with the Course not only more convinced of the truths of the Christian Faith but also more grateful for God's gift of making me a member of the Catholic Church. Helen and Bill did not have this gift. Others had it and lost it. Evelyn Underhill in *Mysticism* observes that it is of primary importance in spiritual matters to be guided by the Church.[4] If one is not a member of the Church, she observed, it is extremely helpful to be guided by the members of some Christian fellowship, one's praying community, which can alert the individual to the shoals of subjective disaster and even to the possibility of going over the deep end. It also became eminently clear to me that a Christian can never gain anything by substituting personal spiritual insights for the traditional guidance of Church teaching. What benefit can one gain by comparing his faith with what he may learn from what appears to be a private revelation? When all is said and done, *A Course in Miracles* has apparently helped many people who knew next to nothing about Christian theology. However, it has confused Christians who did not use it wisely, subjecting its teachings entirely to the truths of faith. Had it not become a cult, *A Course in Miracles* might have been useful as symbolic poetry. This would have permitted the reader to be guided by the truth of faith at all times. Unfortunately, I have seen people who were believing Christians become so intrigued by the beauty of some of its ideas that they made shipwreck of their faith. A helpful religious experience for some became a stumbling block to many, especially those who in these troubled times were shaken in their faith.

Unfortunately, after long experience I must say that it is my conviction, that this Course is a false revelation in the sense that I have defined the term. It has also become a spiritual menace to many.

[4] *Mysticism* (New York: Meridian Books, World Publishing Co. 1974), 105. Cf. the whole chapter "Mysticism and Theology", 95–124.

The reaction to *A Course in Miracles* on the part of the New Age devotees has been predictably enthusiastic. This reaction is typical of much of the New Age spirituality. Rather than try to describe the whole New Age, I will focus on the Course because I am familiar with it. It is written in powerful language, and this is not surprising since its author was a brilliant and respected writer in her own professional field. One of the obvious features of movements like the New Age in the past has been that their followers were attracted by high-sounding language. Saint Augustine recalls that the writings of the Manicheans, a pseudo-mystical movement of his time, were intriguing and high sounding.[5]

A Course in Miracles makes few explicit moral demands beyond forgiveness, which is presented not as an ethical imperative but rather as the road to peace of mind. This is a decent but secondary motive for the disciples of Christ, who must forgive because God has first forgiven us. The reality of sin, which is described as a transient or passing phenomenon, is denied as is the reality of all life's pains and indignities. This is very attractive to those who inhabit the glitzy suburbs of modern cities where one avoids squalor and social injustice. Sin in all its hideousness is replaced by this motto: Eat, drink and be merry, because tomorrow we can't die but will just pass on to nicer things. It was, in fact, Helen's husband who early on pointed out to me this unflattering aspect of the Course's appeal. Perhaps the most damning criticism of the Course is its anemic picture of Christ.

[5] *Confessions,* book III, vi.

None of us has a completely accurate picture of Christ; it is not possible. But the Christian Faith and the Scriptures present all that is necessary. The kindly, luminous, and airy picture of the Christ of the Course is only half the picture. One may be so attached to this consoling vision that one may forget the Christ who preached the Sermon on the Mount and who warned of eternal loss; the Christ who in agony sacrificed his life on the Cross for the salvation of the world. In a recent critical assessment of the New Age, Douglas Groothuis listed some of the Course's theological errors and absurdities.[6] I suggest that those who are interested in *A Course in Miracles* review his assessment. Among other things, it will answer the question: "Why is *A Course in Miracles* one of the bibles of the New Age?"

The Angry Revelations

From all of this one may learn to identify other, more traditionally-grounded alleged revelations that are candidates for the *false* revelations label. Recall that most, if not all, of these reports will be presented by devout Catholics or members of Evangelical or Eastern Orthodox denominations. Frequently these alleged seers can be categorized as super-critical, which usually means that they spend a great deal of time complaining about the errors and vagaries of thought which abound in many religious denominations at the present time. Frequently these visionaries have at hand a great collection of horror stories suggesting

[6] Douglas Groothuis, *Revealing the New Age Jesus* (Downers Grove, Ill.: Intervarsity Press, 1990).

that most of the Church, including many of the bishops, are on the slippery slope to hell. Unlike the followers of *A Course in Miracles,* they are very aware of their anger and rage. They enjoy it. Consequently, they hardly ever appear depressed, because their anger is expressed. They are not quietly coping with repressed anger by covering it over with great bouts of depression. They are up and at 'em.

Their vision of heavenly beings, especially of Our Lord and, if they are Catholics, of the Virgin Mary, is the exact opposite of the New Age Christ. The Lord is coming, and he is coming with an axe. The incredible blend of saccharine images of the Blessed Mother and the dire warnings that all but a few are going plumb to hell are the obverse of the New Age's false Christ. The one thing that they have over the New Age is a very powerful countercultural criticism which makes them a bit more interesting than the mawkish disciples of Mother Earth. In a simple way they present a world vision similar to that of the writer Georges Bernanos, in his mysterious work *Under the Sun of Satan,* a picture of the world in which the loving Savior is apparently defeated by the forces of evil.[7]

It must also be said for the disciples of the angry God and the anguished Virgin that they are Christians in the sense that they believe in all the doctrines of the Church. But they have an incomplete vision of Christ, an angry one which reflects their frustrations and desperation. Forgiveness is not their strong suit, and some followers of these angry people have actually moved away from them because of their

[7] Georges Bernanos, *Under the Sun of Satan* (New York: Pantheon Books, 1949).

complete ignoring of the counsel of Christ: "Judge not, and you shall not be judged" (Mt 7:1).

Like the disciples of the New Age and many followers of *A Course in Miracles,* angry visionaries and their disciples have a problem way down inside with accepting leadership. This is often referred to in psychology as an "authority problem". Like the New Age devotees, they cherish private revelations and their special, personal direct line to God. Although ostensibly convinced of the validity of ecclesiastical authority, they insist that it must agree with them. If they are Catholics, they are professedly pro-papal, but they criticize the Pope and his representatives continuously. The controversy that presently rages among the devout over the consecration of the world to the Immaculate Heart of Mary as requested by the visionaries of Fatima is a good example of their basic antiauthoritarian bias. At times the criticism of ecclesiastical authorities who attempt to control expressions of popular devotion that have become infantile or unbalanced reflects the same distaste for guidance from the community of believers (in the case of Catholics) that one finds in the New Age. It could be a sobering thought that some of the New Age devotees and some angry Christians may share the same digs in Purgatory because they will all be there to learn the same basic lessons that they missed in this world.

The Revelation Addicts

Beyond these two camps, one finds another, namely, those addicted to private revelation. These are the people we have alluded to before who are just plain scared and looking for some direct reassurance from God. They avidly collect all reports of visions and revelations and are generally willing to be guided by the Church in most matters except for the authority of these visions.

As I indicated above, I believe (with human faith, remember) that the loving Divine Being does use private revelation given just for the purpose of encouragement. Lourdes, Knock, Guadalupe, and many other approved revelations served and still serve just this function. I also believe that the Lord can send warnings to an age that certainly could use plenty of warning. I assume that this need has been fulfilled by the Weeping Virgin of La Salette in the nineteenth century and the somber message of the Virgin of Fatima in our own time.

I am open to considering new private revelations seriously. Who am I to suggest to God when and how he will make himself known? I think it is the height of incredible opacity to reject a reported revelation simply because one does not agree with its content, so long as it is not doctrinally erroneous or, clearly, mentally unbalanced. God has never consulted men, nor is there any evidence that Christ fitted his teaching to what people wanted to hear.

But there are groups of good souls who make themselves sitting ducks, as it were, for the possibility of deception by false revelations. They are too curious. They are addicted to possible revelations. Instead of spiritually imbibing the gentle but strong message of Scripture and even of approved revelations, they weekly or monthly find new ones. I suspect that now and then they may come across an authentic private revelation, but they never have the chance to learn anything from it, because they just move on, seeking desperately for some other sign to reassure themselves. They must represent in the contemporary world the same group of people whom Our Lord admonished when he spoke of those who said of the Messiah, "Here he is, there he is. . . . He is in the desert" (Mt 24:23–26).

The Magical Christians

There is yet another group, none of whom is likely to read this book. They are the seekers for magic. Their religious instincts are at a very primitive level, although they have some faith they are unable to differentiate it from primitive religious impulses. Although they will use the symbols of traditional religion, they are actually using them magically. They have no thought of accepting God's will or trusting him. They know exactly what they want, and they are going to get it one way or another.

If these people are the simple, uneducated souls one often finds in large immigrant slums of industrial cities or in villages tucked away in the Third World, one can look with compassion on such impoverished ideas and try to help them grow. But generally one should not attempt to put a new patch on an old garment. Surely in the life of Christ one sees such people appeal to him for healing. His kindly treatment of the Syrophoenician women or his use of a mud paste to heal the blind man indicate that he was willing to meet people where they were and move them along. However, Christ was not a magician. Mysticism, as Evelyn Underhill points out, is the opposite of magic.[8] The mystical is literally the un-

---

[8] *Mysticism,* 70–71, and chapter 7 "Mysticism and Magic".

seen reality. (The Greek root of this word comes from the verb which means to close one's eyes). Magic is what appears to be, but is not. In modern sophisticated society, magic is understood to be simply a sleight-of-hand trick. In primitive situations it is an attempt to make some power beyond oneself subservient to one's purposes. It is unquestionably true that the primitive need for magic survives. One sees it not only in primitive religious behavior but in contemporary attitudes toward medicine and even toward financial institutions and life insurance. Very educated people often show real tendencies toward magical thinking. A well-known biblical scholar, Morton Smith, who recently died, was famous for his interest in magic and his theory that Jesus Christ was a magician. He also suggested that the twelve apostles were a clandestine homosexual society. Another world-famous biblical scholar is said on reliable information to have spent his last years involved with tarot cards. Both Freud and Jung in different ways gave evidence of personal interest in magic. The need for magic is never far away. Recently, in an exclusive section of Manhattan, a plastic statue of Mary was discovered inside a tree. Immediately a fence covered with devotional pictures (mostly related to private revelations) went up, complete with little crowds of people holding candles, keeping vigil. This accident of nature, a tree growing around a plastic statue, stirred up the need for magic even in a sophisticated neighborhood.

Those interested in private revelation must take care not to be involved in magical ideas. Sometimes the same behavior may be exhibited by two people, wearing a religious medal or a cross; for one it is an informed devotion of piety and faith, and for the other it is simply magic. When affluent people who never attend church, pray, or question the moral propriety of their behavior bury statues of Saint Joseph in the garden of their expensive suburban homes in hope of selling them faster or for a better price, we are dangerously approaching magic. When the Missionaries of Charity put a medal of Saint Joseph near a building they hope to get to care for the poor, and back this act of devotion up with piety and perfect abandonment of God's will, it is not magic but an expression of devotion. I have heard those who absolutely deplore devotions to the saints as magic quote the Bible in a clearly magical way. A well-known fundamentalist minister in New Jersey quoted the Book of Kings in a newspaper ad to squelch charges of serious misconduct by a public official, as if these quotations pertained to this official directly. Magic, like taxes, will apparently be with us to the end.

Eight

DEALING SENSIBLY WITH AN ALLEGED PRIVATE REVELATION

As we have seen, the religious discord observable among believers both clerical and lay along with the cultural confusion of our times have caused much uncertainty. I believe that this has given rise to a plethora of reports of private revelations and extraordinary phenomena. What is one to do with all these reports? The two easiest responses—skepticism on the one hand and unbounded credulity on the other—are both unintelligent when one considers all the authentic as well as fraudulent revelations of the past. The truth is to be found between skepticism and credulity. This is not an easy path to walk. The following suggestions are culled from many informed writers, especially Poulain, and may prove helpful.

1. Remain Calm and Discerning

A calm approach is wise but difficult to maintain in the face of a report of a private revelation. Those who have embraced the reported revelation will think you sinful and hardhearted for not accepting it immediately. "Would you reject the Blessed Virgin?" This is a typical challenge. "You know what happened to the scribes and Pharisees, don't you?" That response is a little nasty, but not unusual. There will be a tendency for the very well-intentioned and devout to start a stampede for public acceptance of the reported revelation. Then those who are trying to remain calm and discerning may react with annoyance and decide for subjective reasons to discount the whole thing. The words of Rudyard Kipling come to mind: "If you can keep your head when all about you are losing theirs, then you are a man" (or a woman). The awesome thought that you might possibly be dealing with another Bernadette should lower your blood pressure considerably and assist you to remain objective.

2. Learn As Much As You Can before Making Any Judgment

One must learn as much as possible about the recipient of the supposed revelation. This is often difficult to do, and yet no rational judgment can be made without this knowledge. The credulous rarely ask questions seriously, and if they do, they are satisfied with the knowledge that their visionary is very devout or perhaps a member of a religious community. The charlatan, Magdalena of the Cross, was thought by almost all to be a devout nun, and yet she was apparently possessed by the devil. Such questions as the following may prove helpful in learning about the person.

What is the education of the recipients? What do we know of their previous life? Have they ever been emotionally disturbed? Were they devout? Were they involved in works of charity and generosity? If not, after their supposed revelation took place, did they change? What were their relationships with others? Is there any evidence that they were seriously seeking a spiritual life? When they were children and adolescents, were they at least devout or well-behaved? If not, did their experience cause them to change their behavior? These questions do not all have to be responded to with positive answers, but they are obviously important in assessing the credibility of recipients.

QUESTIONS REGARDING ALLEGED RECIPIENTS' RESPONSES TO THE REPORTED REVELATION

Has this experience powerfully shaped the life of individual recipients causing a kind of conversion or new depth of piety? Have they responded with humility and docility to advice and spiritual counsel, or have they resisted? Have they become self-important givers of prophetic knowledge and attempted to surround themselves with publicity? Or have they tended to be reserved about their experience, like Bernadette and the children of Fatima? Did they profit financially or by favors of wealthy people as a result of the revelation, or has their lifestyle remained substantially the same as it was before? Have they been anxious to be accepted and to have their message proclaimed, or have they been willing to leave all this in the hands of others? If there has been any undue publicity or unwise disclosure, have they been regretful? Or have they been led by others whose discretion may be questionable in this instance?

Have the subjects made an authentic text or description of the revelation available? Have they cooperated with legitimate Church authorities in preparing a report? Does the revelation contain anything that is contrary to the Catholic Faith, or that is absurd? Is the content totally unoriginal and, therefore, possibly derived from other private revelations, or is it simply a rehash of traditional teaching? If the content is familiar, does it have distinct features, like the testimony of the children of Fatima that Russia would be converted? Are the distinct features related to something in the actual everyday experience of the recipient or are they generally unforeseen and unexpected? Does the revelation contain predictions of future events? Does it contain ways of speaking or systems of logic that may open it to a theological or moral misunderstanding? Or, on the other hand, does it simply seem to be a restatement of things well known? Finally, does it represent the opinion of the alleged visionary restated in a way as to give it the authority of the Divine Word? (This kind of thing is often observed in long accounts contained in books supposedly dictated by a heavenly teacher.)

We have seen earlier in this work that no report of a revelation is free from subjectivity and, consequently, from the possibility of distortion or misunderstanding from several sources. Because of this, one should not come to a final conclusion about the verity of the revelation, even if there are minor difficulties which do not seriously distort its overall meaning. As mentioned already, Pope Benedict XIV gave examples of several revelations which received general approval for private devotion (for example, those of Saint Hildegard) and which had details that were neither accurate or approved. Also, we see in the case of Saint Catherine of Siena that some of her reports of revelations may not be acceptable, even though she is a great mystical writer and Doctor of the Church. Since he lived many years in a most active ministry, many opinions are quoted of Padre Pio without documentation or details of the context. Such quotations may have an interest, but should never be taken as the precise intention of the saintly padre, much less as a revelation. Even mystics are entitled to their own private opinions and prejudices.

If you find your head spinning with all of these questions (and there are even more), at least this exercise will make you aware of the complexity of the question, "Is this an authentic revelation? Did God directly, or indirectly through a heavenly figure (perhaps Our Lady), speak to this particular person, and did the person get the message right?" How often people short-circuit this process of evaluation by appealing to the occurrence of apparent miracles associated with the revelation. This approach frequently raises more questions than it answers.

ARE THERE REPORTED MIRACLES AND
WHAT DO THEY MEAN?

It is not difficult to find reports of miracles or at least of cures and healing associated with an alleged revelation. The excitement and attention that a private revelation causes may attract many who are very understandably seeking help from God for some illness or problem that is beyond their ability to cope with.

Indeed, an authentic miracle is a sign of divine revelation, and this is clearly seen in the Old and New Testaments. That these signs and wonders were part of the gospel message and of its verification cannot be denied, according to many theologians, including the statement recently made by Pope John Paul II.[1] However, not every healing or cure is a certifiable miracle, that is, one useful in verifying the authenticity of a revelation. The present definition of miracles required for a process of canonization includes the following elements: the instantaneous or very rapid disappearance of life-threatening or very serious physical symptoms, previously empirically verified (for example, by X-rays), without adequate medical treatment, without scientific explanation, and without recovery period or relapse. It also requires the judgment of an experienced medical panel convened by the local bishop to certify that a cure

[1] John Paul II, *Wonders and Signs,* introduction by Benedict J. Groeschel (Boston: Daughters of St. Paul, 1990), 63 ff.

medically fills the above requirements, and this is only done after some years of good health and good conduct by the person who has been cured. If the cured person has sought gain or notoriety, the cure is simply not considered. Of the immense number of cures that have happened and have been reported at Lourdes, fewer than 80 have been certified by the bishop because of the stringency of these requirements. If a miracle occurred in conjunction with a particular revelation, it would probably be years before this could be ascertained by ecclesiastical authority. There are, in fact, many cures of physical and mental illness that are not certifiable because of lack of documentation, lack of empirical evidence (as in the case of psychological and moral cures like severe addictions), and even because of circumstances like the large number of reports. Consequently, most healings that are reported as a result of a special manifestation of God's power are not certifiable and therefore not useful for validating a private revelation. When reported by sane and sensible witnesses who are not given to undue enthusiasm and who have no personal investment in the revelation, such healings can be cumulatively considered as interesting signs. They simply merit our interest and consideration as part of the total picture.[2]

CAN PARANORMAL PHENOMENA BE REGARDED
AS MIRACULOUS EVIDENCE?

Certain events—for instance the spring flowing at the hand of Bernadette in Lourdes, the appearance of a

[2] Cf. Sr. Briege McKenna, *Miracles Do Happen* (Ann Arbor, Mi.: Servant Publications, 1987).

whirling sun observed by thousands at Fatima (including skeptics and unbelievers)—are properly called paranormal experiences. Frequently there is apparently no known explanation in physics or psychology to account for these phenomena. Because of the possibility of deception or even of diabolical influence in paranormal phenomena, the Church has never used them in deciding the authenticity of a private revelation. This reluctance will seem incredible especially to those who have observed some of these phenomena (and I know many well-balanced people who have). However, in the scientific study of these phenomena it is clear that they often occur in the lives of people who are not saintly or devout in any way consistent with Christianity. As Bernard Ruffin points out in his biography of Padre Pio, the lives of Helena Blavatsky, Rudolph Steiner, Edgar Cayce, and even Rasputin abounded in paranormal phenomena, and they were not saints.[3] Consequently when these signs are associated with a revelation, they should be considered interesting but never the basis of a certain judgment about its validity. As someone open to the possible miraculous origin of some of these phenomena I cannot agree with the enthusiasts that weeping icons, moving statues, and even extraordinary solar manifestations are in the category of evidence. Obviously, these things have a great impact on those who have observed and experienced them firsthand. They should feel perfectly free to arrive at their own subjective certitude and even to share it with others. But they are not justified in obliging others to accept their testimony.

[3] Ruffin, *Padre Pio: The True Story,* 2nd ed. (Huntington, Ind.: OSV Press, 1991), 398.

Certain photographic phenomena are particularly popular in attempts to verify a doubtful apparition. Photographs reportedly showing angels, apparitions, visual symbols, and other peculiar things abound, especially in cases where there is no ecclesiastical approval. Those impressed by these things would do well to examine the reproduction of similar photographs presented as part of the comprehensive study of parapsychology by the distinguished psychological manualist Dr. Benjamin Wolman.[4] Again it must be said that these experiences may be far more convincing to those who have personally witnessed them, but they should not be taken as a source of certitude.

A word must be said about moral cures that occur at places associated with revelations. Priests will often report that they were deeply affected by the piety of pilgrims confessing and receiving the sacraments at a place associated with a reported revelation. I have had this experience myself, and it certainly can affect one's attitude and objectivity. The reality of the grace-filled response of pilgrims and of those associated with the reported revelation, like the staff, directors, and even visionaries themselves, is deeply moving and a genuine religious experience in its own right. I suggest that only those who have been to such a place of pilgrimage should make a judgment about these experiences. I am sure that even in the case of a false revelation—even if it be fraudulent—many people have had genuine religious experiences that may even have been a source of healing. This has been observed tragically in the case of those who in the past or even recently discovered that they had

[4] Benjamin Wolman, ed., *Handbook of Parapsychology* (New York: Van Nostrand Reinhold, 1977).

been duped by false prophets. Each person's religious experience stands alone. The fact is that we cannot judge the reported revelation by its fruits. You would be required to take Joseph Smith and the Mormon doctrine very seriously if you went simply by the effects of his revelation. It is responsible for several billion dollars in religious donations every year—and yet very serious questions have been raised by Mormon scholars about the moral life of this "prophet".[5]

Some Conclusions from the Above

I. DO NOT MAKE HASTY JUDGMENTS ABOUT ULTIMATE AUTHENTICITY

If you are inclined to accept a reported revelation, there is no need to arrive at total conviction about it. (Remember you should never believe any private revelation as you do the truths of the Faith.) It is wise to make the resolution to say repeatedly that you were favorably impressed, that you profited by the expression of faith, that you found the writings devoutly helpful, but not that you believed. Resist those, even the visionaries, who demand total conviction. Recall Saint Elizabeth of Schoenau and her interviews with the relics of Saint Ursula. She demanded absolute belief.

[5] See Fawn M. Brodie, *No Man Knows My History: The Life of Joseph Smith* (New York: Alfred A. Knopf, 1946).

2. WHILE COLLECTING INFORMATION SUGGESTED ABOVE, RESIST THE TEMPTATION TO CONSIDER ANY PIECE OF EVIDENCE AS ULTIMATELY CONCLUSIVE

This is a wise resolution even if you observed some of the inexplicable phenomena or a healing yourself. Usually Catholic revelations are related to Our Lady or to a saint. Be satisfied to place your conviction in the known and accepted devotion to this saint and listen with interest to the reported revelation concerning the person. For example, in the case of a reported Marian apparition, focus your attention and faith on the words of Our Lady in the Gospel of Saint Luke—words which must be accepted by any believer: "All generations shall call me blessed."

3. DO NOT AVOID THE CONSIDERATION OF AN HONEST CRITICAL EVALUATION SO LONG AS IT IS NOT MOTIVATED BY PREJUDICE

It is strangely observable that the reports of alleged revelations attract prejudiced people, that is, those who prejudge, or judge before the facts are known. All shrines appear to have their friends and foes. The friends refuse to hear criticism and the foes refuse to hear anything good. An absurd example of hostile prejudice against a revelation was the attempt of the French novelist, Émile Zola, to kidnap a woman who had been healed at Lourdes. It has been my observation that those opposed to a revelation are often victims of pre-existing prejudice, such as pseudo-scientific attitudes against any miraculous phenomena, hostility to the form of piety expressed at the event, and so forth. This kind of hateful response may lead to character assassination and calumny. If one must be careful not to be carried along by the credulous, one must also resist the contrasting incredulity. The skeptical inquirer may not be any more objective than the devotee.

A Few Short Cuts

The rules suggested above may be augmented by some simple considerations which permit an open-minded observer to dismiss a reported revelation without doing too much investigation. It may be stated explicitly that one must be certain that at least one of the following factors is involved in the reported revelation. Reported revelations can be dismissed in the following cases if one factor is certain:

1. The recipient or seer is clearly mentally ill, or the revelation contains psychotic details. Naturally, one must ignore the bias of those who reduce all revelations of God to hallucinations. They are simply prejudiced.

2. The substance of the revelation is clearly contrary to the public divine revelation and the teaching of the Church. Since revelations are usually vague and almost never stated in theological terms, it may take some time to deduce this. A revelation of a fourth person in the Godhead would justify such an immediate judgment. The recent report of a visionary that aborted children are reincarnated, if accurate, would immediately disqualify the alleged recipients because reincarnation is contrary to Catholic faith.

3. The reported revelation, while not heretical, is clearly inconsistent with the teaching of the Church.

For example, the revelation contains an accusation of sins and possible defamation of character without proof other than the words of the visionary. Many pseudo-mystics have announced the damnation of their critics.

4. An obvious attitude on the part of the alleged visionary which is defiant, proud, judgmental, or provocative is enough to discount the alleged report. On the contrary, one should expect to find self-abasement, according to Saint Teresa.

5. Erroneous prophecy, when it is given to support the supposed revelation, is a good sign that one is dealing with something less than the power of God. Along with immediate prophecies of the end of the world, there is the fantastic case of the anti-pope Benedict XIII, the last of the Avignon anti-popes, who accepted the prophecy of an abbot who assured him that he would triumph over all his opponents. The abbot had predicted the totally unforeseeable event that the anti-pope was going to arrive at the abbey by ship when he was not expected. The poor old anti-pope, on the basis of this apparent fore-knowledge, accepted the abbot's prophecy that he would be accepted as the true Pope and rejected the citation of the Council of Constance. He died de-posed and in exile, thus ending the Great Western Schism (1422).[6]

6. Poulain suggests that the individual who has received the revelation should be open to the possi-bility of self-deception. Because of the simplicity of some recipients, they may not understand this pos-sibility and may see it as an infidelity to their mission.

---

[6] Cf. A. Poulain, *Graces of Interior Prayer* (London: Routledge and Kegan Paul, 1950), 357.

An educated person who reports a vision should be able to face the possibility of self-deception. The failure to do so may suggest paranoia.

7. Evidence that the reported revelation or the recipient is involved in magic, the occult, or the diabolical is sufficient reason to discount the report at once. Most religiously aware people will be immediately sensitive to and repelled by the magical and the occult. Even when these supposed recipients of messages from another world are devout or religious, informed believers at least instinctively draw back. The poorly informed and unprepared—and unfortunately their number grows daily—will not be able to distinguish the spiritual from the psychic. If a question occurs, obviously believing experts familiar with both psychic phenomena and the mystical should be consulted because the psychic or even the occult may appear to be miraculous. A good rule of thumb is that the inexplicable is not necessarily divine or supernatural.

The tragic case given above of Magdalena of the Cross, who deceived thousands, including theologians and prelates, for thirty years apparently by the power of the devil, should be sufficient warning to all of this real possibility. In these skeptical times one may hear clergy disparage the idea of a personal evil spirit, but they do so in the face of Scripture, Tradition, and dogmatic teaching. As recently as 1972 Pope Paul VI spoke of the necessity of accepting the reality of diabolical spirits and their influences.[7] Satanic cults abound in the Western industrialized nations as well as in the so-called Third World. On the

[7] General Audience, Nov. 15, 1972, *L'Osservatore Romano* (Nov. 23, 1972): 3.

other hand, one may commit a serious injustice by accusing a reported visionary of diabolic influence without sufficient evidence. Even the presence of apparent diabolical influences around the site of the reported vision does not warrant the judgment that the origin of the revelation was diabolical. In fact, the opposite might be conjectured if the location has become a site of great faith and fervor. In any case, the possibility of manipulation or interference by diabolical forces must never be ignored. Simply put, clear evidence of an involvement of the reported recipient of the revelation in anything savoring of the occult or diabolical is sufficient reason to discredit the entire report.

Obviously in all of life's situations where judgments are difficult to make, caution, deferring of judgment, hesitation, and collecting comprehensive information are necessary. This is certainly the case in the matter of reported revelations. No one should feel guilty about being cautious, even if one is positively disposed to the message or the revelation. Intelligence, judgment, and discernment are all gifts of God and should be used. The historical attitude of the Church reflected in the frequently maligned cautions of the hierarchy is sufficient justification for resisting those demanding complete acceptance of their own pronouncements. As we have seen in the case of approved revelation, many of the clergy who were cautious and even doubtful eventually became powerful witnesses to the validity of the visionaries' claims. They ultimately served the cause of truth well, and those who condemned their initial caution did them an injustice.

The most difficult task remains for the devout believer who accepts the possibility of private revelation and has an informed opinion that this particular revelation at hand may be valid and in fact a gift from God. Like most intelligent and virtuous positions in life, progress is along a knife's edge, avoiding credulity and skepticism. If time proves the revelation authentic, false, or ultimately doubtful, the person who has followed a reasonable middle road will have served the Kingdom of God well.

Nine

GUIDELINES FOR SPIRITUAL
DIRECTORS

The considerations given so far are meant for the
believers who are interested and concerned to respond intelligently to reports of possible revelations.
The following suggestions are given for those who
are dealing in a professional way, as clergy, spiritual
directors, or even physicians and therapists, with
those who believe they have been favored with a
special grace or who are deeply and emotionally
involved in revelations given to someone else. There
are devout souls whose primary interest in life has
become the publication of a reported revelation or
the biography of a saintly person apparently en-
dowed with supernatural gifts: for example, those
deeply involved in the revelations made at Fatima
or in the life and words of Padre Pio—to mention
two popular causes which have already received
much approval. As a rule, once a revelation is completed and finally approved the number of people so
singularly involved declines as in the case of Lourdes
and Guadalupe. There is no longer a need to spread

Note: The reader who does not direct individuals may pass on
to chapter ten.

the message, although thousands, even millions, continue to benefit by it. A similar phenomenon occurs in the cases of servants of God after beatification and canonization. Once finally approved the cause of a saint or the popular interest in the shrine will become integrated into the life of the Church and will no longer be the consuming interest of a limited circle of devotees. Our concern in this chapter is to address the responsibilities of those who come on the scene early and who have to make crucial decisions about the authenticity of the case.

Be Well-Informed

The first and most urgent suggestion for directors is to read and study the best classical literature on the subject of revelations. One needs to be armed with some of the key concepts we have discussed already. The relationship of the subjective and objective elements in perception and inner experience must be thoroughly understood. The possibility of mystical ideas which are unconsciously arrived at as creative expressions of the mind must be grasped and must be differentiated from private revelations properly so called. Experiences like those of Anna Katharina Emmerich, María of Ágreda, and even Helen Schucman must be understood. Even though they were very different (since Dr. Schucman was not a well-instructed Christian or Catholic at all as the others were), they all experienced their literary endeavors as something they did not apparently cause or control. They all believed their ideas came from divine inspiration. The insights of Evelyn Underhill and Friedrich von Hügel are very helpful in understanding this phenomenon. [1]

The teaching of the Church, especially the principles enunciated by Pope Benedict XIV and summarized here, should be well understood. An informed familiarity with both Saint John of the Cross and Saint Teresa of Avila is invaluable. The recent book *Fire Within* by Father Thomas Dubay is an excellent introduction. [2] The "Rules for Discernment of Spirits" by Saint Ignatius Loyola are also most insightful, although these rules usually have been subsumed by other writers like Poulain. [3] The possibility of distortion, error, or even innocent self-deception needs to be grasped in its entirety. In writing the following suggestions for directors (from now on this comprehensive term will be used for all professionals involved), I will assume all that I have written above as a given. The following suggestions can only be understood in that context.

Be Patient and Gentle

Those personally and intimately involved with a possible revelation will not be objective or perhaps even

[1] E. Underhill, *Mysticism* (New York: New American Library, 1974), and Friedrich von Hügel, *The Mystical Element in Religion* (London: James Clarke, 1961). Underhill's chapter on visions and voices is most illuminating and much more easily available than von Hügel's great work.

[2] Thomas Dubay, S.M., *Fire Within* (San Francisco: Ignatius Press, 1989).

[3] Cf. A. Poulain, *Graces of Interior Prayer* (London: Routledge and Kegan Paul, 1950), 638–42.

capable of working toward objectivity. An appeal should be made for caution and patience, and the possibility of deception should be explained. The director may have to be very patient in working toward some objectivity on the part of the individual. The threat of withdrawal by the subject from the director because he is proceeding cautiously should not become a tool of manipulation. Such attempts on the part of the recipient of the alleged revelation are very negative signs, though not conclusive.

The director must try to discern if such a negative response is a result of simplicity and naïveté, of pride, or of both. Recourse to severe measures, like absolute commands and directives that the individual cannot understand, are usually counterproductive. This is especially true in a time like our own when all are raised to be self-expressive and self-directed. While such coercive techniques may have worked in earlier times, recourse to them now may suggest that the director is either insecure or lacking in patience and empathy. Direct commands can only be used as a last resort and usually terminate the relationship with the person who is seeking assistance.

Be Objective

Poulain suggests that a director display *no admiration* for the reported revelations, even if he suspects that they are authentic.[4] This is a solid principle consistent with contemporary theories of counseling. The director cannot afford to become a devotee or disciple of the person being directed. This would establish a

---

[4] Ibid., 380.

kind of contract that would impede the director from being objective. While the recipient of the alleged revelation may really need others to be supporters and sympathizers and even helpers, this person needs the assistance of an objective director most of all.

Be Cautious Where Others Are Involved

If the experience reported only results in an increase of devotion and love of God on the part of the recipient, then it is enough to see that this person is not emotionally carried away and stays on a normal, sane path through life. In the case of inner words or locutions, it is worthwhile to note that Saint John of the Cross suggests that they simply be "given no heed".[5] He suggests being guided in all things by reason and what the Church has taught and teaches every day. If the recipient is simply encouraged but not led to action by such vivid experiences, it does not seem necessary to point out all the dangers except to warn against pride and vanity. When the recipient feels compelled to share experiences with others, a director would be very wise, after reviewing all the cautions listed above, to seek consultation with learned and prudent people informed on the spiritual life and open to the possibility of the existence of private revelation. There are always people around who are learned in other areas, but totally uninformed about private revelation, and consequently not much help. These are likely to spend much time

[5] A thorough discussion of this matter is contained in *The Ascent of Mt. Carmel* by Saint John of the Cross, books 2 and 3. A good summary of his teaching and of Saint Teresa's is contained in Dubay, *Fire Within*, 14.

seeking some other explanation from psychology and parapsychology rather than directly considering the case at hand. If the report of this revelation is going to affect the life of the Church, and it is hard to see how it would not, notification should be made first to ecclesiastical authorities and their advice should be sought. However, such information is usually automatically classified as dangerous, and those in authority tend to avoid danger instinctively. They often have good reason to do so. Directors may not find much objective help from officialdom, and may in the course of time find that they are accidentally drawn into a controversy from which personal reputations may never recover. It is generally seen as very bad news for officialdom when it is reported that Our Lady has appeared to someone. One can be sympathetic to officials who already have more trouble than they can handle. Anticipating the negativism of officialdom may be helpful for the director who is trying to remain objective.

Even more caution is necessary when some work is suggested by the revelation, such as building a shrine or starting a new devotion. Those who believe that they have received such a revelation must be tested for patience over a period of time. God does not rush. The director would do well to recount the experiences of those who received such instructions in the past. Poulain offers as an example the case of Saint Juliana of Mont-Cornillon, near Liège in Belgium (1192–1258). She had a revelation instructing her to work for the establishment of a feast in honor of the Blessed Sacrament, but she did not present this instruction to theologians for almost twenty years. She encountered only opposition and persecution with her attempts to reform the convent where she served as superior. Eventually she had to leave and wandered for twenty years until her death. Only long after her death did her revelations get any real hearing, because a priest whom she knew in Liège became Pope Urban IV. The Feast of Corpus Christi was finally celebrated in the universal Church over one hundred years after Saint Juliana had her revelation.[6]

This account should discourage all but the most convinced that a very strong sense of reliance on Divine Providence is necessary for all involved, especially the alleged recipient. I would be inclined to think that a sense of urgency or hysteria on the part of the supporters or the recipient is an indication that the revelation will come to little or nothing. On the other hand, a sense of persistence and trust in God's providence is a very encouraging sign. Obviously one only has to think of the pathetic picture of Joan of Arc at the stake, or of Bernadette being told that she was useless to her religious community to appreciate the meaning of patience and trust.

Be Discerning

The director should carefully observe if the recipient or the supporters are certain that they are not victims of illusion. Poulain mentions that this certain conviction is one of the best ways to insure being deluded. A frank openness to the possibility of illusion is a very good sign. Poulain mentions sadly that María of Ágreda considered herself protected from error and believed that it was a sin not to share her conviction.[7]

---

[6] Poulain, *Graces of Interior Prayer*, 357–58.
[7] Ibid., 359.

Although Dr. Helen Schucman often disagreed with the contents of what she wrote, she indicated to me that she did not feel that she could correct any of her writings because they came from above. This would be a very painful situation for anyone, but especially for a very complex and forceful personality like Dr. Schucman.

A confessor who has the authority to do so should require a manifestation of conscience, that is to say, total honesty about the inner dispositions of the subject. A director with some other role, for instance, a religious, or lay counselor, may request the equivalent, total candor and honesty. If it becomes clear that this disposition is absent, that the director is only being told a part of the occurrence, and that things are being left out, the director should question whether it is wise to give any further time and attention to the case.

The desire for further revelations or spiritual favors is a very bad sign. Christian spirituality is directed toward greater selflessness. Such self-centered desires are a sign of not only spiritual immaturity, but also of growing egotism. Certainly this is not what special grace is about.

Another sign suggesting false revelation is of the recipient's insistence that the decisions of others must be made on the basis of what is allegedly revealed to the visionary. Saint Teresa gives a splendid example of just the opposite behavior. Saint Teresa founded the Carmelite reform partly because of a private revelation, in fact, because of what seemed to be an order from the Lord himself. However, when she approached the Dominican theologian Ibáñez for advice, she did not give him any such reasons, but only the personal concerns and motives that she had as an individual.[8] Spain had been filled in those times with pious fanatics who preached their alleged revelations, including the notorious Magdalena of the Cross. Saint Teresa who speaks so often of revelations, did not seek to impose hers on others.

A particular nuisance is the supposed visionary or one of the disciples who reports a revelation condemning the director or others for not accepting their story immediately at face value. This supposed divine threat is not uncommon and seems to be a certain sign that one is dealing with a false, if not fraudulent, revelation. Poulain gives the following insight which is worth quoting, since this kind of arrogance of mistaken seers and their followers is not uncommon, despite its obvious distastefulness and lack of charity. Speaking of a visionary who had threatened him in Paris, he writes:

> Finding myself exposed one day to this class of menace, I quietly replied: "Such words are a sign that your revelations are not from Heaven. The spirit who speaks to you does not know my interior dispositions. He is not aware that I *sincerely* wish to obey God, and that if I am exacting with regard to proofs it is *from a sense of duty,* in order to avoid illusions. God cannot threaten a man who acts from such motives; He ought to do so, on the contrary, if I committed the imprudence of believing you on your word alone. And, further, it is you that He should blame, for if I am without proofs, it is because you do not furnish me with that of sanctity.
>
> The spirit responsible for the revelation (if there was one) felt that he had been unskillful. For in the next communication he took my side, declared that I was more than right, and that I was indeed a saint. He

[8] Ibid., 384.

promised to supply, but *at a later date,* proofs that would be *irresistible,* I am still awaiting them; and yet the seer has left this world![9]

Be A True Spiritual Guide

The first purpose of spiritual direction is not the discernment of visions and interior words, or appraisal of such things. The primary purpose is to assist another in the arduous road to holiness, in fact, to that transforming union with God which is the eternal destiny of all human beings. Nor is it the task of a priest or any other person put in the role of spiritual guide simply to support and facilitate the activities of those who are involved in proving an alleged revelation. No pastor or spiritual director can afford to lose sight of the responsibility for objective judgment. If a director is invited to participate only as a consultant and supporter of the supposed recipient, he is in a very vulnerable position. The same is true of a priest or religious who is simply chaplain for a group dedicated to supporting and disseminating the revelation.

The spiritual integrity of the Church must be safeguarded; this requires that the goal of salvation and sanctification be kept clearly in mind. It is an unfortunate fact that in many religious activities and projects, the ultimate goal is obscured or even lost. In projects as varied as social service and education, health care, and even liturgical life or founding a religious community, we may allow the ultimate goal of Christianity—the glory of God through the

[9] Ibid., 387.

sanctification of his children — to be obscured or even forgotten. However, there is a special insidious danger in activities related to a possible private revelation. Since it is assumed that the messages are direct actions of God, those claiming to be entrusted with these messages may begin to see themselves or be seen by others as speaking for God. If this were purely and simply the case (and as we have seen, even in the most approved revelations it cannot be the case), we could defer the consideration of personal striving for holiness because it would be subsumed by the revelation itself. Indeed, we may assume that in Jesus' dealing with the apostles and disciples, every act and thought contributed to their salvation and spiritual progress. There would be no need even to allude to the responsibility for personal striving. But this is emphatically not what we observe in the gospel. He continuously directs, instructs, admonishes, corrects, and even scolds them: "What have you been talking about on your way along the road?" (Lk 24:17), "How long should I put up with all of you?" (Lk 9:41), and "Seek first the Kingdom of God and his justice" (Mt 6:33).

These and many other quotations make it clear that Our Lord took on the responsibility of directing and encouraging his followers in overcoming selfishness and in growing spiritually. Even though he himself was the revelation, he taught his followers the ways of holiness, humility, patience, forgiveness, generosity, prayer, and many other disciplines while establishing the beginnings of his Church.

I have observed at times that directors, coordinators, chaplains, and spiritual assistants of all kinds are extremely reluctant to confront the recipient of an alleged revelation with the principles of the spiritual

life. They are understandably intimidated by the recipient and cajoled by the disciples. The magnificent
examples of such great mystics as Saint Teresa and
such remarkable visionaries as Saint Bernadette contrast with this attitude. They were both anxious for
any counsel or instruction that would lead them on
the road to holiness. They were far removed from the
attitudes of those who feel themselves so favored that
they can only instruct others and never learn themselves. The director should be careful not to put
himself accidentally in the situation of being a servant
and not a guide. That would be a forgivable but
nonetheless false and fruitless humility.

It is worth noting briefly that several informed
spiritual authors on the subject also warn the spiritual
director against being emotionally drawn in by the
supposed recipient of the revelation. This warning
could be expanded to all those who are involved in
the intensely personal and emotionally charged atmosphere surrounding a possible revelation. Those
individuals, even if they have never met the assumed
visionary (who by this time may be dead) share a sort
of secret knowledge of which the rest of the world is
oblivious. This awareness of secret knowledge (called
arcana) generates a sense of comradeship and special
importance. The disciples quickly become spiritual
brothers and sisters. The director should be careful
that this intimacy not become something unworthy
of the spiritual intentions which have brought the
group together. The belief that all involved have a
special divine call or destiny will inevitably lead them
to be deluded into thinking that all they do or express
is virtuous, that they are all under a charmed star.
Such thinking is simply an opening to spiritual ca-
tastrophe and to the very painful disedification of

others. This disconcerting phenomenon of the infallible elite can be observed in movements as different as the early Franciscan spirituals and some of today's encounter groups.

Conclusion

The director of a possible recipient of a private revelation and, to a lesser extent, the spiritual guide of a group involved with a reported revelation are not to be envied. If Divine Providence puts the task before you of guiding someone who is involved in possible revelation, you must recognize the gift of a heavy cross. To do this task well, one needs intelligence, diligence in study, patience, an ability to accept unjust criticism, clearheadedness (really a logical mind), and all the moral and theological virtues and gifts of the Holy Spirit. One must be prepared from the outset for the likely and disappointing discovery that there has been accidental deception, misunderstanding, spiritually disguised egotism, and even (rarely) fraud. The supposed visionary may be totally sincere and subjectively honest, yet may have experienced one of those automations (unconsciously self-directed experiences) spoken of by Poulain, Underhill, and many others. The subject may be truly virtuous and even a saintly soul, but mistaken.

I cannot imagine why anyone would want the arduous task of being a spiritual director in the case of a private revelation. A priest or someone with pastoral responsibilities may be obliged to take up such a burden in particular circumstances. To seek out such a role seems to me to suggest a craving for self-importance, masking feelings of inadequacy, or perhaps a masochistic need to suffer. If indeed the revelation is true, then Divine Providence may be assumed to be leading the chosen soul. If it is not true but the person is deeply sincere, surely the good God will send some guide along the way to cushion the blows of disappointment and humiliation that the individual will suffer. I would immediately have questions about the judgment, if not the motives, of someone who anxiously volunteered for such a task. Those who have taken up such causes as promoting a devotion or the reputation of a supposed visionary must always keep this work subsidiary to their over-all Christian and pastoral responsibilities. And let them ask for many prayers and humbly beg God for much more enlightenment.

Ten

A WORD TO THOSE WHO THINK THEY HAVE RECEIVED A REVELATION

I have deliberately put beyond the scope of this book any real advice or counsel for those who think they have received a private revelation. Because of the danger of self-delusion, people in this situation need a director and not a book. The following few suggestions are given not to substitute for direction and wise counsel but to serve more as a caution. They may also be read with profit by those who are interested in possible revelations.

Along with finding a wise and informed director and being candid and docile to him, it is imperative for the subject to mistrust the supposed revelations in general, and even if one is convinced of their reality, at least to mistrust one's own interpretation of them. Saint John of the Cross sums up a great deal of experience and wisdom in the following paragraph:

> Let us conclude then with this precaution necessary for the avoidance of any delusion or hindrance from these variously caused locutions: We should pay no heed to them, but be only interested in firmly directing the will through them toward God; we should carry out His law and holy counsels perfectly—for such is the wisdom of the saints—content with knowing the mysteries and truths in the simplicity and

verity with which the Church proposes them. An attitude of this kind is sufficient for a vigorous en-kindling of the will; hence we do not have to pry into profundities and curiosities in which danger is seldom lacking. St. Paul in regard to this conduct states: *One should not have more knowledge than befits him* (Rom. 12:3).[1]

One is also very well-advised, if one believes that a revelation has been given, not to desire or ask for any more. Writing of interior locutions Saint John of the Cross comments: "No soul who does not deal with them as the work of an enemy can possibly escape delusion in a greater or lesser degree in many of them." Poulain is strong in suggesting that the recipients avoid giving consultations of any kind based on their revelations. Such simple-minded appeals as, "Ask Our Lady if my son should get married to his girlfriend", are the very stuff that illusions are made of. The well-advised will avoid such things and limit themselves, if they must say anything, to observations and advice gained from the Gospels. An answer like the following is perhaps appropriate: "If she is a good girl and they are really ready to marry, it might be wise to think about the possibility."

Poulain suggests, following Saint Teresa and Saint John of the Cross, that it is wise, at least in the beginning, to repel revelations. If they have a prophetic quality to them and predict future events, the subject should write the revelation down explicitly and see if the events happen exactly as they were led to believe they would. Any miscalculation or mistake would suggest subjectivity and even illusion.

[1] St. John of the Cross, *Ascent of Mt. Carmel,* trans. Kavanaugh and Rodriguez (Washington, D.C.: ICS Publications, 1973), book II, chapter 29, 207.

Another cheerful quotation from Saint John of the Cross may be a salutary slap in the face to someone who seeks the new revelation: "On judgment day, God will punish the faults and sins of many with whom He communed familiarly here below and to whom He imparted much light and power. For they neglected their obligations and trusted in their converse with Him."[2]

A Simple Rule

Is there a simple rule for those who believe they have experienced revelations? Yes, I think there is. Like all truly universal things, this rule may be despised because it is commonplace. For example, those seeking some secure road to physical or spiritual health may dismiss as commonplace such basic suggestions as eating proper food, getting sunlight and exercise, or, in the case of the spiritual life, prayerful reading of the Scriptures every day. They want something special like Naaman the leper who disdained the waters of the Jordan which could have cured him. The commonplace but essential protection of all who believe that they have been gifted with a private revelation is humility. Yes, that! Saint Teresa summed it up well.

> The good or the evil does not lie in the vision but in the one who sees it and in whether or not she profits by it with humility; for if humility is present, no harm can be done, not even by the devil. And if humility is not present, even if the visions be from God, they will be of no benefit. For if that favor

[2] Ibid., book II, chap. 22, no. 15, 185.

which should humble a nun when she sees she is unworthy of it makes her proud, she will be like the spider that converts everything it eats into poison; or like the bee that converts it all into honey.[3]

Humility will lead the way to patience, as it did for Saint Juliana; the way to obedience, as it did for Saint Teresa; and the way to divine love, as it did for Saint Francis.

[3] St. Teresa of Avila, *Collected Works,* vol. 3, trans. K. Kavanaugh and O. Rodriguez (Washington, D.C.: ICS Publications, 1985), 140.

Eleven

A SAFER WAY —
RELIGIOUS EXPERIENCE

Almost all devout people have religious experiences or times of heightened awareness of God's presence and power. Except in times of special trial called "aridity", these experiences are something we come to rely on without being very aware of it. They are like days of good weather and sunlight. We take them for granted and only notice when they are missing.

I am aware that the very impulse that causes some to look for revelations and unusual signs is present in many, perhaps most, religious people to some degree. The longing for solace, certitude, charity, the loving encounter with God whom we seek to love, all impel us to make the awesome request of Moses, "Let me see your face."

The fact is that God does make his presence known to us in innumerable ways, as we have seen. He gives us his word in Scripture, his presence in the sacraments, his appeal in the needy. Christ assures us that he is present with us till the end of the world. What we really need is not extraordinary signs of this presence in visions and revelations, but a sense of reverent attentiveness to this religious experience as it comes to us in ordinary ways. Like most of the people in Jerusalem and Galilee two thousand years ago, we pass Christ and do not recognize him. This unfortunate fact was so clear to Saint Augustine that he poignantly wrote, "The only thing I really fear is Jesus passing by." Let us for a moment examine the idea of ordinary religious experience.

Depending on our personality and preferences, these experiences may be more intellectual, more emotional, or more aesthetic, that is, related to our sense of the beautiful. For example, one person may get very taken up with thinking about the truths of salvation or even about some profound fact directly related to his own life, perhaps a truth that led to conversion. Others may be feeling loneliness and a sense of rejection. The belief that Our Savior personally loves them, his words "Come to me and you will find rest", deeply penetrate the darkness they experience. They feel emotionally relieved and no longer isolated and rejected. God is very present to them. This is a very real religious experience and has sustained millions of people in difficult times.

Still others are bored and tired of the humdrum of life, of the gross materialism of the big city. They start to feel like cogs in a wheel, like things rather than persons. On the way home from work they stop into a quiet church for a few minutes of silence. There, surrounded by majestic architecture and perhaps the solemn tones of an organ, they forget all the ugliness outside. The majesty and splendor of God are reflected in the beauty of his temple. They become quiet and are restored as persons. They remember their individual relationship with the Heavenly Father, or pause to pray at the shrine of the Blessed Mother. "I am real again." I have witnessed many city-worn people in Saint Patrick's Cathedral having just this beautiful experience, which is neither intellectual nor emotional but rather a sense of holy beauty. Another may have the same experience walking quietly in the woods and in the fields.

What are these experiences and many others like them? For the believer they are the experience of the presence of God in his own life. Faith tells us that God, the Creator, is always present. But so also is his Son, the Redeemer: "Behold I am with you." And so is the Sanctifier: "I will send you another advocate who will remain with you."

The transcendent reality of God is always around us, although we are unaware of it most of the time. This is because the complex mechanism of our emotional and intellectual lives, as well as the intrusion of everything else we encounter, draws our awareness from the reality of God's presence. The distractions that come into our minds in everyday life caused the poet Wordsworth to complain, "The world is too much with us." This awareness of too much intrusion and at the same time of the presence of God behind all of life has caused people to wander into quiet places, woods and mountains, or into retreats, monasteries and ashrams throughout the world. There, in the silence, people led by the words of scriptural revelation or of some sacred texts of their own religion have sought to know God, not by words but by experience.

This experience has some things in common with the private revelation we have been discussing, and yet there is a difference. It is similar in that it is illuminating—an inner event, a happening all of its own, quite distinct from the external activity that may be associated with it, such as participation in a religious service. Of course one can perform a religious service reverently and yet at the same time be open to inner religious experience, so that the two become integrated.

Religious experience is also like private revelation in that it is a distinct inner experience, although not as vivid. Perhaps the most obvious difference between the religious experience and private revelation is that the latter gives the impression of being quite beyond the control of the individual. If I go into church to pray and feel God's presence I must choose to respond. I must relax and take my time, and, in a more fervent experience, I must turn my will and all my powers of mind under voluntary control to the act of worship and praise. In a revelation there is a sense of an intrusion, which one welcomes but does not cause. Even though there may be elements in religious experience that I am certain do not come from my conscious mind or will, I am aware that it is *my* experience. It is quite different from meeting *another* who might come into my life unexpectedly and independently. It is subjectively quite different from welcoming an unexpected visitor at the door or receiving an unexpected phone call. That kind of experience is alien to my intentions, it comes from outside me. A real private revelation is that kind of experience. The visitor, as it were, is coming independently of one's awareness or expectation. Simply put, religious experience as distinct from private revelation is recognized immediately as highly subjective. The difference between the two experiences can be shown in the two following citations: the first is a citation from a letter to her superior by Saint Thérèse and describes a religious experience (in this case, primarily an intellectual one):

"Oh what a comfort it is, Mother, this way of love! You may stumble on it, you may fail to correspond with grace given, but always love knows how to make the best of everything; whatever offends our Lord is burnt up in its fire, and nothing is left but a humble, absorbing peace deep down in the heart.

I can't tell you how much illumination I've found before now in the works of that great father of ours, St. John of the Cross. When I was seventeen or eighteen, it was all the spiritual food I needed. After that, I found that all spiritual books left me as dry as ever, and I'm still like that. I've only to open one— even the finest, even the most affecting of them—to find my heart shut up tight against it; I can't think about what I'm reading, or else it just gets as far as my brain without helping me to meditate at all. I can only escape from this difficulty of mine by reading Holy Scripture and the *Imitation of Christ;* there you have solid, wholemeal nourishment. But above all it's the Gospels that occupy my mind when I'm at prayer; my soul has so many needs, and yet this is the one thing needful. I'm always finding fresh lights there; hidden meanings which had meant nothing to me hitherto. It's an experience that makes me understand what's meant by the text, *"The Kingdom of God is here, within you"*. Our Lord doesn't need to make use of books or teachers in the instruction of souls; isn't he himself the Teacher of teachers, conveying knowledge with never a word spoken? For myself, I never heard the sound of his voice, but I know that he dwells within me all the time, guiding me and inspiring me whenever I do or say anything. A light, of which I'd caught no glimmer before, comes to me at the very moment when it's needed; and this doesn't

generally happen in the course of my prayer, however devout it may be, but more often in the middle
of my daily work.[1]

An intensely different quality of expression is to be
found in Bernadette's original description of the first
apparition at Lourdes. There is a totally different
feeling. The experience comes from without. It is
indeed a vision and the beginning of a private revelation:

> I put my hand in my pocket, and I found my rosary
> there. I wanted to make the Sign of the Cross. . . . I
> couldn't raise my hand to my forehead. It collapsed
> on me. Shock got the better of me. My hand was
> trembling.
> The vision made the Sign of the Cross. Then I tried
> a second time, and I could. As soon as I made the
> Sign of the Cross, the fearful shock I felt disappeared.
> I knelt down and I said my rosary in the presence of
> the beautiful lady. The vision fingered the beads of
> her own rosary, but she did not move her lips. When
> I finished my rosary she signed for me to approach;
> but I did not dare. Then she disappeared, just like
> that.[2]

The vision of Bernadette, totally unexpected and
never altered in any of her testimony, is something
clearly outside herself. It is not primarily subjective.

There is an experience that seems to fall between
the two, between the obvious personal experience of

---

[1] St. Thérèse of Lisieux, *The Story of A Soul: Autobiography of
Saint Thérèse of Lisieux,* trans. Ronald Knox (Glasgow: Font
Paperback, William Collins and Sons, 1987), 174.
[2] René Laurentin, *Bernadette of Lourdes* (Minneapolis: Winston
Press, 1979), 27–28.

Thérèse, in which emotion, will, and intelligence are completely involved, and that of Bernadette. A similar experience but one difficult perhaps to categorize, falling, as it were, between the two and lacking the overwhelming response described by Bernadette, is given by a young woman, then a Protestant who later became a Catholic spiritual writer and theologian of great intellectual acumen. This woman, Adrienne von Speyr, recognized as something of a genius, recorded the following account of what was either a vision or a very powerful religious experience at the age of fifteen. Since she wrote this account later, one may suppose that some subjectivity unconsciously entered into her description.

In the same month of November 1917, I awoke very early one morning—it was barely even light—because of a golden light which filled the whole wall above my bed. And I saw the Mother of God as in a picture, surrounded by various people (these were standing somewhat further back while she was right in the foreground) as well as by several angels, some of which were as big as she was, others as small as children. The whole thing was like a picture; yet the Mother of God was alive, in heaven, and angels were changing their positions. I think this lasted for a long time; I gazed as in a wordless prayer and was overwhelmed with admiration; never had I seen anything so beautiful. In the beginning all of the light was like brilliantly sparkling gold, then it slowly faded, and while it faded the features of the Virgin Mary became more prominent. I was not frightened in any way, but rather filled by a new, strong and very tender joy. Not for a moment did the whole thing strike me as unreal; it did not occur to me that I could be the victim of an illusion.

> If I remember correctly, I did not tell anybody about it except Madeleine, to whom I reported the event as something quite natural. Mad simply replied, "I would have liked to have seen her too." We never talked about it again. The memory of this vision remained intensely alive for me.[3]

In no way do I want to pass judgment on this account of a writer of such acumen, but it is possible that her memory was augmented by details learned later on from Catholic piety, since the description of the vision is so predictable. The fact that at the time of the vision she was a Protestant with little or no contact with Catholicism is what is so interesting in this report.

These descriptions, especially that of Saint Thérèse, serve to illustrate that religious experience of a type very different from private revelation is possible to all. Over the years I have collected over two thousand reports of religious experience from students in courses on spirituality. Many of these students first said that they had had no religious experience, because they thought it had to be something like what happened at Fatima or Lourdes. Often older Catholics immediately refer to the powerful film, *The Song of Bernadette,* when asked for an example of a religious experience. When I noted that this film depicted a private revelation and explained the real meaning of the term religious experience, all but a handful were able to describe, in rather vivid detail, experiences of the presence of God in their lives. They were able to do this even if it happened decades before.

[3] Hans von Balthasar, *First Glance at Adrienne von Speyr* (San Francisco: Ignatius Press, 1968), 115–16.

Our lives are engulfed in experience—some religious and some neutral and some sadly sinful. Some of these are very weak and easily forgotten—for example, pleasant conversation with the clerk at the food store. Others are strong and memorable—seeing an automobile accident. The same is true of religious experience: a quiet prayer in the evening, when one easily responds to the truth of faith that Christ, forgiving and gentle, is with us at the end of the day, will easily be forgotten. Another religious experience in an intense moment of life will remain engraved on our memory. Sometimes it is because of the historical circumstances, such as a prayer said when the attempt was made on the life of the Pope in 1981. Other religious experiences will be remembered because they had a vibrant quality all of their own—intellectual, emotional, aesthetic, or a blend of two or three of these. These should be recalled occasionally. These experiences are grace-filled without being private revelations. They are a fascinating conjunction of the grace of God with the rich inner life of the individual.

The following experience was written by a German Protestant theologian, Jurgen Moltmann. It illustrates all too well how human life and need can come together with grace. I choose this experience because it is so dark in its beginnings. It starts in hell—hell created by the Nazis, the worst possible situation—and shows how God's graces are given to a young man caught up in this horror.

The university entrance exam—was put forward so that we could be sent to the guns, as Air Force auxiliaries. At that time I really wanted to read mathematics and physics at the university. The "iron rations" in the way of reading matter which I took with me into the miseries of war were Goethe's poems and the works of Nietzsche. In February 1945 I was taken prisoner by the British, and for over three years I was moved about from camp to camp in Belgium, Scotland and England. In April 1948 I was one of the last to be "repatriated", as the phrase went.

The break-up of the German front, the collapse of law and humanity, the self-destruction of German civilization and culture, and finally the appalling end on 9 May 1945—all this was followed by the revelation of the crimes which had been committed in Germany's name—Buchenwald, Auschwitz, Maidanek, Bergen-Belsen and the rest. And with that came the necessity of standing up to it all inwardly, shut up in camps as we were. I think my own little world fell to pieces then, too. The "iron rations" I had with me were quickly used up, and what remained left a stale taste in the mouth. In that Belgian camp, hungry as we were, I saw how other men collapsed inwardly, how they gave up all hope, sickening for lack of it, some of them dying. The same thing almost happened to me. What kept me from it was a rebirth to new life thanks to a hope for which there was no evidence at all.

It was not that I experienced any sudden conversion. What I felt all at once was the death of all the mainstays that had sustained my life up to then. It was only slowly that something different began to build up in their stead. At home, Christianity was only a matter of form. One came across it once a year at Christmas time, as something rather remote. In the prison camps where I was I only met it in very human—all too human—form. It was nothing very overwhelming. And yet the experience of misery and forsakenness and daily humiliation gradually built up into an experience of God.

It was the experience of God's presence in the dark night of the soul: "If I make my bed in hell, behold, thou art there." A well-meaning army chaplain had given me a New Testament, I thought it was out of place. I would rather have had something to eat. But then I became fascinated by the psalms and especially by Psalm 39: "I was dumb with silence, I held my peace, even from good; and my sorrow was stirred" (but the German is much stronger—"I have to eat up my grief within myself"). . . . Hold thou not thy peace at my tears; for I am a stranger with thee, and a sojourner, as all my fathers were." These psalms gave me the words for my own suffering. They opened my eyes to the God who is with those "that are of a broken heart". He was present even behind the barbed wire—no, most of all behind the barbed wire. But whenever in my despair I wanted to lay firm hold on this experience, it eluded me again, and there I was with empty hands once more. All that was left was an inward drive, a longing which provided the impetus to hope. How often I walked round and round in circles at night in front of the barbed wire fence. My first thoughts were always about the free world outside, from which I was cut off; but I always ended up thinking about a center to the circle in the middle of the camp—a little hill, with a hut on it which served as a chapel. It seemed to me like a circle surrounding the mystery of God, which was drawing me towards it.

This experience of not sinking into the abyss but of being held up from afar was the beginning of a clear hope, without which it is impossible to live at all. At the same time, even this hope cut two ways; on the one hand it provided the strength to get up again after every inward or outward defeat; on the other hand it made the soul rub itself raw on the barbed wire, making it impossible to settle down in captivity or come to terms with it.

God in the dark night of the soul—God as the power of hope and pain: this was the experience which molded me in what are a person's most receptive years, between 18 and 21. I am reluctant to say that this is why I became a Christian, because that sounds like joining a party. Because I believe that I owe my survival to these experiences, I cannot even say I found God there. But I do know in my heart that it is there that he found me, and that I would otherwise have been lost.[4]

How different from the experience of Adrienne von Speyr at fifteen. But one thing is in common. Both were completely unexpected. To use C. S. Lewis' expression, they were both "surprised by joy".

Moltmann's account simply describes an experience of grace—a call of God in the heart. It has none of the aspects of a vision or of a private revelation, although it had a profound effect on his life. None of the precautions of Saint John of the Cross against "visions" is pertinent in this case. In fact, this kind of experience is what John of the Cross seems to approve of while very suspicious of what we have called private revelations and extraordinary experiences. He would have been much more at ease with Moltmann's account than he would with the one described by von Speyr. This, however, does not in any way call into question the honesty of von Speyr's account, or the verity of her experience.

One of the most powerful and historically important religious experiences in Church history is the conversion of Saint Augustine, described in the *Con-*

[4] Jurgen Moltmann, *Experience of God* (Philadelphia: Fortress Press, 1980), 7–9. (Used with permission of Augsburg-Fortress Press.)

fessions (book VIII, 7). After reading Romans 13:13, Augustine had no vision or locution or direct experience of a revelation. It was a personal internal response to grace. "For in that instant, with the very ending of the sentence, it was as though a light of utter confidence shone in my heart, and all the darkness of uncertainty vanished away." This is a powerful human experience but devoid of any suggestion of anything like a private revelation. Anyone really interested in religious experience should read book VIII of the *Confessions*.

Religious Experience As a Way to Grow

Perhaps the most powerful religious experiences come from our contacts with others. We may experience the presence of God in the face of a saint or holy person. We may find the face of Jesus imprinted like the image in the legend of Veronica, on the tortured features of a dying person. We may simply be consoled by the smile of someone who cares when we are troubled. Sometimes these memories remain in our minds as vividly as a vision or apparition. On the other hand, they give us a kind of certitude about God's care and presence in our lives, but they spare us the temptation to pride and self-importance that may accompany extraordinary revelations or paranormal experiences.

As we have seen, most of the well-known and authenticated visions occurred to simple people, usually children, who are not looking for anything like this at all—for instance, the children of La Salette and Fatima, or Saint Bernadette. Others were simply folk who were praying, like Saint Margaret Mary or Saint Catherine Labouré, or the peasant people of Knock, in Ireland. They had not thought of ecstasy, but, to use the words of Saint Thérèse, were only expecting the monotony of sacrifice. When these special graces came to them, they often opened the door to much suffering and dislocation in their lives.

The best lesson one may learn from these authenticated and canonized visionaries is to do what you are supposed to do and leave the rest to God. The fulfillment of duty is the guiding principle of any decent moral life, in any religion of the world, because it expresses the natural law and is completely consistent with the revealed law of God. The fulfillment of duty placed before us by the providential circumstances of life, as we are guided by the commandments and the teaching of the gospel, is the straight road to God. Along that road any valid religious experience which occurs may be useful.

I am astonished when I see so many sincere Christians missing the powerful experience of the presence of Christ in the world because they are afraid or disinclined to find him where he teaches that he can be found, namely, among the poor.

When I was thirteen years old, I was taught a poem in school that would guide my entire life; I can still hear Mother Dolorita reading this poem to us in class. As I listened to the words, I knew that this poem would be very important in my life. It was as significant to me as any apparition I might have received. It is not only a beautiful poem and almost unknown, although written by Longfellow, but it contains the message of this chapter more eloquently than any words of mine. If you are one who looks for signs of God, for some of his footprints in the world (to use the words of Saint Bonaventure), then you might find it very helpful to meditate on this poem.

THE LEGEND BEAUTIFUL

"Hadst thou stayed, I must have fled!"
That is what the Vision said.

In his chamber all alone,
Kneeling on the floor of stone,
Prayed the Monk in deep contrition
For his sins of indecision,
Prayed for greater self-denial
In temptation and in trial;
It was noonday by the dial,
And the Monk was all alone.

Suddenly, as if it lightened,
An unwonted splendor brightened
All within him and without him
In that narrow cell of stone;
And he saw the Blessed Vision
Of our Lord, with light Elysian
Like a vesture wrapped about Him,
Like a garment round Him thrown.

Not as crucified and slain,
Not in agonies of pain,
Not with bleeding hands and feet,
Did the Monk his Master see;
But as in the village street,
In the house or harvest-field,
Halt and lame and blind He healed,
When He walked in Galilee.

In an attitude imploring,
Hands upon his bosom crossed,
Wondering, worshipping, adoring,

Knelt the Monk in rapture lost.
Lord, he thought, in heaven that reignest,
Who am I, that thus thou deignest
To reveal thyself to me?
Who am I, that from the centre
Of thy glory thou shouldst enter
This poor cell, my guest to be?

Then amid his exaltation,
Loud the convent bell appalling,
From its belfry calling, calling,
Rang through court and corridor
With persistent iteration
He had never heard before.
It was now the appointed hour
When alike in shine or shower,
Winter's cold or summer's heat,
To the convent portals came
All the blind and halt and lame,
All the beggars of the street,
For their daily dole of food
Dealt them by the brotherhood;
And their almoner was he
Who upon his bended knee,
Rapt in silent ecstasy
Of divinest self-surrender,
Saw the Vision and the Splendor.

Deep distress and hesitation
Mingled with his adoration;
Should he go, or should he stay?
Should he leave the poor to wait
Hungry at the convent gate,
Till the vision passed away?

Should he slight his radiant guest,
Slight this visitant celestial,
For a crowd of ragged, bestial
Beggars at the convent gate?
Would the Vision there remain?
Would the Vision come again?
Then a voice within his breast
Whispered, audible and clear,
As if to the outward ear:
"Do thy duty; that is best;
Leave unto thy Lord the rest!"

Straightway to his feet he started,
And with longing look intent
On the Blessed Vision bent,
Slowly from his cell departed,
Slowly on his errand went.

At the gate the poor were waiting,
Looking through the iron grating,
With that terror in the eye
That is only seen in those
Who amid their wants and woes
Hear the sound of doors that close,
And of feet that pass them by;
Grown familiar with disfavor.
Grown familiar with the savor
Of the bread by which men die!
But to-day, they know not why,
Like the gate of Paradise
Seemed the convent gate to rise,
Like a sacrament divine
Seemed to them the bread and wine.
In his heart the Monk was praying,

Thinking of the homeless poor,
What they suffer and endure;
What we see not, what we see;
And the inward voice was saying:
"Whatsoever thing thou doest
To the least of mine and lowest,
That thou doest unto me!"

Unto me! but had the Vision
Come to him in beggar's clothing,
Come a mendicant imploring,
Would he then have knelt adoring,
Or have listened with derision,
And have turned away with loathing?

Thus his conscience put the question,
Full of troublesome suggestion,
As at length, with hurried pace,
Towards his cell he turned his face,
And beheld the convent bright
With a supernatural light,
Like a luminous cloud expanding
Over floor and wall and ceiling.

But he paused with awe-struck feeling
At the threshold of his door,
For the Vision still was standing
As he left it there before,
When the convent bell appalling,
From its belfry calling, calling,
Summoned him to feed the poor.
Through the long hour intervening
It had waited his return,
And he felt his bosom burn,
Comprehending all the meaning,

When the Blessed Vision said,
"Hadst thou stayed, I must have fled!"
Henry Wadsworth Longfellow
From Tales of a Wayside Inn[5]

Although this poem speaks of a private revelation or vision it is very clear that the message of the poem is related to the real world. Unlike so many private revelations, it did not lead the monk to self-importance or pride, but rather to the most profound humiliation. He questions himself, his own motives, his sincerity, and despite all of this, he is consoled by God.

The importance of the principle enunciated, namely, to serve God where one is commanded to serve him, in this case in the poor, is the road to real spiritual growth. The importance of this fact has been constantly engraved on my mind for many years because of this poem. The following is one of the most powerful experiences of my entire life. If I may ask the reader to bear with it, the importance of ordinary religious experience will become obvious.

"I Was in Prison"

When I was a very young priest, I was assigned to work at Children's Village, in Dobbs Ferry, New York, a treatment center for emotionally disturbed boys. It often happened that my work took me to the prisons in New York where some of the boys had relatives and where some of them eventually ended up themselves. The prison that I went to

[5] Henry W. Longfellow, *The Poetical Works* (London: Collins Press, n.d.), 361–64.

most frequently was a huge, stainless steel cage in Brooklyn, then called Atlantic Avenue Jail. I often went there in the middle of the day to visit inmates. As is the custom in the Capuchin order, I wore a brown Franciscan robe. One afternoon the guards invited me to have a bowl of soup with them while the inmates were being counted and were locked in their cells. In the middle of lunch, a guard came running in and said, "Father, please come upstairs quickly. A boy just hanged himself." We ran up the stairs and down to the end of the cellblock, where a number of inmates and correctional officers were gathered together. As I approached I saw the young man with Hispanic features lying on the floor. They had torn off his shirt and were giving him artificial respiration. He was very thin and had a short black beard. As I knelt down next to him, the prison doctor said, "It is all right, Father, he just knocked the air out of his lungs. He tried to kill himself, but the belt broke. He is all right; go back and finish your lunch."

The thought passed through my mind: How could he possibly be all right? He had just attempted to kill himself. Gradually, as I knelt there, the boy came to, and one by one the inmates and the correctional guards walked away. Eventually, I was kneeling there with two guards and the doctor, and the boy was regaining consciousness. As he opened his eyes, he focused on my face. He smiled at me—a beautiful smile. He had a look of recognition on his face and appeared to be waiting for me to say something to him. In a moment I realized to my horror that this boy thought he was dead. He had hanged himself and had opened his eyes to see a man with a red beard and a long robe leaning over him.

In my consternation, I moved my head to the side so that he could see some of the officers and the doctor. A look of incredible sadness came over his face. He realized that he was not dead, that he had not escaped, that they had brought him back to serve a long sentence in prison (he had been one of the accessories in a hold-up in which someone had been killed). He was looking forward to twenty years in prison.

As the boy regained full consciousness, he began to cry, deep pitiful cries. Everyone left us completely alone sitting there on the cellblock floor. He cried and cried. He could not escape.

As I sat there on the floor with him, I realized that this young man had been mistaken about whom he had seen when he opened his eyes, but I was not mistaken. It was very clear to me whom I was seeing. I could feel the pounding of the nails, I could smell the sweat and blood, I could hear the cry, "My God, why have you forsaken me?" Never before had the words of Christ in the Gospel of Saint Matthew been so real to me. "I was in prison and you came to me."

This short account can hardly communicate the impression that the experience left upon me. It was no miraculous experience. There was no sound from on high, there was no vision or awareness of something from another world. Far from being something that would cause me to be proud or think that I was important, this experience was profoundly humiliating. Although it happened twenty-five years ago, it is burned into my mind and comes back to me so often. It fits in perfectly with the poem by Longfellow. It does not call me to self-adulation but rather to humiliation and repentance.

. . . had the vision
Come to him in beggar's clothing,
Come a mendicant imploring.
Would he have knelt adoring
Or have listened with derision,
And have turned away with loathing?

This kind of religious experience is perhaps the best. It is founded on the reading of the gospel and on the good example of people from my childhood who took care of the poor. It reminds me of the generosity of my own parents to needy neighbors; it reminds me of the sisters I had in school, most of whom showed a real interest in those who were unfortunate. Some of those women were outstanding in their concern for the needy. It brings together the ordinary events of life and transfuses them with the light of divine grace given through the gospel, the Church, and the sacraments.

Your Own Experience

Everyone reading this book has had some remarkable religious experiences in life. Remarkable, but not extraordinary. Unfortunately, we tend to overlook them, to forget them, to tuck them away, to allow them to lapse into oblivion. And yet, they are the words of God spoken to us as real as the words spoken to Abraham, Moses, and Saint Paul. In an age that looks for reassurance from God, it might be very wise for Christians meditatively to pay closer attention to their own religious experiences. Of course they are pedestrian; of course they are not unusual; of course they call us to do things of a humdrum nature that we don't want to do. A thousand times in the last twenty-five years this experience in the prison has caused me to become involved with people who, humanly speaking, were not going any place and who would never be able to respond adequately to what I was doing for them, or even to understand why I was doing it. The words of Saint Thérèse, in a letter to her sister who had gone to Lourdes, explain very well the value of such a call, "To ecstasy I prefer the monotony of sacrifice."

The nature and meaning of religious experience is something I hope to explore in another longer work. For the present moment it is sufficient to suggest that you write down one or two of your own strong religious experiences. They are usually very clear in your mind, like pictures taken with a flashbulb. You may remember details which are unimportant. These experiences may be weak or powerful, filled with joy and sorrow, wonder or fear, meant either to heal or to wound. They powerfully shaped who you were and who you are right now. They are experiences of God and should never be overlooked. For those with a taste for the extraordinary, they may suggest a safer way.

GLOSSARY OF TERMS

Some Surprises

This glossary of terms relating to alleged revelations and visions could be called a glossary of surprises. It is given here not only to assist the reader but also to be a guide to other texts on the subject. Most glossaries are a bit dull and we skip over them; this one is not dull. I have purposely used classical authors to emphasize how often our ideas about these phenomena are completely inadequate and open to confusion if not delusion. For example, most of our readers would think that the apparition of Our Lady to Saint Bernadette at Lourdes represents the highest form of supernatural experience. According to such writers as Saint Teresa and Saint John of the Cross (both Doctors of the Church) this kind of extraordinary vision accompanied by an exterior locution represents the lowest form of divine communication. In fact, such a vision can be given by Divine Providence to a random group of very ordinary souls as happened at Knock in Ireland. A supernatural vision may even be given to a sinner to stop him from doing evil. Such a vision is reported to have occurred to a potential assassin of Saint Charles Borromeo as he pointed a pistol at the saint offering Mass in the Church of Santa Maria Dei Monte in Rome. (This event is commemorated by a painting in the church.)

A vision which seems to the individual like the perception of an external object may be an extraordinary act of Divine Providence, but it need not be an extraordinary phenomenon. In the case of Bernadette, the vision certainly was not an external phenomenon because no one else present saw it. We are not able to determine this in the case of the visions of Joan of Arc because no one else was present. In both cases, these visions gave rise to a life of heroic virtue, and the visionaries were eventually canonized. They are not recognized as saints because they received visions but because of their virtue in responding to God's mysterious call.

As we have already seen, great caution must be exercised with reports of visions because self-delusion or even diabolical influence is apparently common in such things. In such cases, faithful recourse to competent spiritual directors and to the pastoral authority of the Church is essential. Father Dubay offers the following pertinent quotation from Saint John of the Cross and his own trenchant observations on it. "Evidently, then, even though the words and revelations be from God, we cannot find assurance in them, since in our understanding of them we can easily be deluded and extremely so."[1] Dubay comments:

> If the history of religion teaches us anything, it is that this sanjuanist caution is entirely correct. The thousands of sects that have sprung up in twenty centuries of Christianity alone are eloquent, even if tragic, witnesses to the vagaries, whimsies and oddities presented to the world in the name of private enlight-

[1] St. John of the Cross, *Ascent of Mt. Carmel,* trans. Kavanaugh and Rodriguez (Washington, D.C.: ICS Publications, 1973), book 2, no. 10, 167.

enments. And history is not able to record the numberless private extravaganzas and blind alleys into which men and women have been and still are led away when they depart from the solidity of the Spirit-indwelt Church to pursue their own personal persuasions.[2]

Thus warned, we proceed to define a few common terms. We are guided in our endeavor by Poulain and Dubay. Anyone more seriously interested in this topic should review both of these writers.[3] Dubay is especially helpful in sorting out nuances between the writings of Saint John of the Cross and Saint Teresa. Unfortunately, it is beyond the scope of this glossary to do this. The more informed reader will find Dubay extremely helpful and enlightening in this regard.

(Note: This glossary is not alphabetical but rather sequential, that is, it may be necessary to read preceding descriptions in order to understand the ones that follow).

Religious Experience

There are many definitions, and even William James did not settle for any one of them. In this book, religious experience means any subjective state suggesting to the individual the presence or action of the divine or transcendent reality. Related but contradictory to this religious experience is an awareness of an evil presence or force which is opposed to the unity, truth, goodness, and beauty of Being.

---

[2] T. Dubay, *Fire Within* (San Francisco: Ignatius Press, 1989), 261.

[3] Cf. Poulain, *Graces of Interior Prayer* (London: Routledge and Kegan Paul, 1950), chap. 20, and Dubay, *Fire Within,* chap. 14.

A. ORDINARY RELIGIOUS EXPERIENCES

Those experiences which occur to an individual in the normal course of life are ordinary religious experiences. The individual is aware that he is responding to some internal or external stimulus and is deliberately associating this experience with religious faith or seeking. It is obvious that one's background and convictions will give shape to one's experience. A Buddhist will ordinarily have an experience consistent with his knowledge of Buddhism. Many visitors to a shrine or place of reputed apparitions will report feeling very close to God, but they do not report extraordinary phenomena. When the experience departs from the expectations and experience of the individual it is de facto extraordinary—for example, the experience of Saul on the road to Damascus or Rabbi Zolli's experience of Christ when he was the leader of the Jewish community in Rome in 1945.[4]

B. EXTRAORDINARY RELIGIOUS EXPERIENCE

The phrase "extraordinary religious experience" describes any perception or awareness of the divine which is not consciously sought by the individual directly or indirectly and which occurs so spontaneously that the individual finds it alien to his own inner functions and awareness. (Alien here means different or distinct from self, not hostile or contradictory.) The experience described above by Adrienne von Speyr is extraordinary, that of Pastor

[4] Tomasso Ricci, "Not Converted but Fulfilled", *30 Days* (April 1991): 68–73.

Moltmann is ordinary, although it takes place in an environment of extraordinary difficulty. Included in extraordinary religious experience are those external phenomena like apparent changes in the sun or lights in the sky, sometimes reported by large numbers of people at places of alleged apparitions. To call something extraordinary, does not imply that it is supernatural, but rather paranormal or outside the parameters of our daily experience.

C. PARANORMAL AND PARAPSYCHOLOGICAL EXPERIENCE

Extraordinary religious experience (and here extraordinary must be a relative term, as is paranormal), hypothetically falls into two categories: 1) *paramystical,* or that which appears to have its origin in some divine or diabolical cause and is so designated because of the circumstances surrounding it, and 2) *parapsychological,* or that which has a cause in nature, but this cause is not now and, in fact, may never be comprehended by the human mind. Many human experiences fall into this category and are amply described by Professor Benjamin Wolman in *The Handbook of Parapsychology.*

Often it is difficult to make a clear distinction between paramystical and parapsychological experiences, and indeed there may be experiences which draw their causality from both sources. An example would be the apparent psychic phenomena described in the life of Saint John Bosco. Some of his dreams and prophecies appear to fit into the realm of the psychic or the parapsychological.[5] But since they

[5] P. Meseguer, *The Secret of Dreams* (Westminster, Md.: Newman Press, 1961).

occurred in the life of a canonized saint where does one draw the line?

Despite the term paramystical, it must be recalled that some experiences may have total or partial natural causality. A case in point may be the occurrence of the stigmata. At times superficial or surface stigmata appear to be a natural phenomenon in the life of a person who may not appear to be devout. At other times medically inexplicable deep stigmata may appear to be miraculous. It is reported that the stigmata of Padre Pio went through his hands.

Paramystical simply means that these phenomena occur in a very religious surrounding or in the life of a deeply religious person. Indeed these experiences may be entirely subjective, products of the unconscious mind, or on the other hand they may be like the conversion of Saint Paul, something that is related entirely to divine causality.

Common Categories of Paramystical Experience

A. LOCUTIONS OR WORDS

1. *Exterior sounds.* These are received by the hearing apparatus of the human ear but they have no apparent physical origin, in fact, they are simply miraculous. This is very rare.

2. *Imaginative words.* These are not the products of what is called the imagination, under the direct control of the individual, but rather they occur in the imaging faculty of the individual. They are quite vivid and in the case of supernatural origin they often contradict the expectations of the recipient. It is crit-

ical to differentiate them from auditory hallucinations (products of serious pathology) and from simple imaginations as may occur in a highly suggestive or histrionic person.

When Saint Bernadette was in a trancelike state at Lourdes, she simply reported instructions as if she had heard them "from the Lady" with her own ears. She "heard" the words but the witnesses did not hear them.

3. *Intellectual locutions.* These are simply the communication of concepts and ideas which can easily be put into words by the individual. The person will say, "I know it to be true." Sometimes this is called "a word of knowledge" by the devout.

In parapsychology the phenomena of *internal dictation* is reported when one knows the sentence one is writing but not the next sentence. *Automatic script* is said to occur when the person is not even aware of the context or of the next word. Saint John of the Cross uses the phrase *"successive locutions"* for intellectual locutions where the individual is conscious of words but does not hear them.

Father Dubay gives the following example in modern terms and then gives us the hard sayings of Saint John of the Cross as a sobering reminder.

A prayerful teacher or student or even letter writer may notice that in a difficult matter a sudden surge of ideas flows easily. One did not know what to say or how to put it, and yet at the moment of composition finds an accompanying enlightenment. While this assisting locution in itself contains no deception, there can be error in the conclusions that the recipient may draw from it. The light given is so delicate that it does not fill the intellect completely, and the person remains free to operate in a merely human manner and thus to misunderstand or to misapply the message or to infer erroneously what does not follow. While successive locutions are surely a blessing in themselves when they come from God, yet John was convinced that misapplication are not rare:

> I greatly fear what is happening in these times of ours; if any soul whatever after a bit of meditation has in its recollection one of these locutions, it will immediately baptize all as coming from God and with such a supposition say, "God told me," "God answered me." Yet this is not so, but, as we pointed out, these persons themselves are more often the origin of their locution. . . . They think something extraordinary has occurred and that God has spoken, whereas in reality little more than nothing will have happened, or nothing at all (*Ascent of Mt. Carmel,* book 2, no. 4–5, pp. 204–5).[6]

B. VISIONS

1. *Exterior visions.* These are also called corporeal or ocular. An object is formed or seems to be formed outside the mind of the person who experiences it with bodily eyes. The clearest example is the simple appearance or vision of the figures at Knock in Ireland. Even those at a long distance saw the light and reflection but had no idea of what they were looking at.[7] Bernadette never questioned that she saw the Lady with her eyes although, in fact, there was apparently not an exterior vision.

[6] Dubay, *Fire Within,* 258.
[7] Mary Purcell, "Our Lady's Silence", in *A Woman Clothed with the Sun,* ed. John J. Delaney (New York: Doubleday, 1961), 147–71.

2. *Imaginative visions.* Like imaginative words these occur in the imaging faculty of the mind. They must be distinguished from visionary hallucinations by reason of their origin which is not from pathology. Most apparitions appear to be of this type although the individual usually accepts them as part of the ordinary visual experience even though they contain unusual details. Often the visionaries report that the vision was extremely beautiful, unlike anything they have seen before. The children of Fatima reported that the Lady they saw was somewhat transparent, "Like a statue made of snow", and "almost made transparent by the rays of the sun".[8] As mentioned above, the French artist Jules Bastien-Lepage used a fascinating technique to illustrate both the clarity and the obscurity of the visions of Joan of Arc.

Many of the experiences of Saint Teresa of Avila are described as unimaginative visions. Often these were unexpected. In the Sixth Mansion of the Interior Castle she writes that "a person is not thinking of seeing anything, nor has any idea crossed the mind when suddenly the vision is revealed in its entirety, causing within the powers and senses of the soul a fright and confusion which soon afterwards changes into a blissful peace." It is extremely important to recall that these vivid visions of the Saint were part of her extraordinarily advanced state of spirituality. (For a catalog of Saint Teresa's visions, see Poulain, pages 302ff.)

3. *Intellectual visions.* These are perceived by the mind alone without any interior image. A remarkable example of such an experience is given by the

---

[8] Cf. S. Zimdars-Swartz, *Encountering Mary* (Princeton, Princeton University Press, 1991), 73; based on *Fatima in Lucia's Own Words,* ed. L. Kondor, (Fatima: Postulation Center, 1976).

Russian Orthodox Archbishop Anthony Bloom. It was the occasion of his conversion. As an atheist, he read the shortest Gospel (Mark) to prove a priest was wrong and became aware irresistibly that Christ was there present in the room, although he could not see him and did not believe in him.[9] Certainly each case must be seriously examined with these categories in mind. At times there will be informed people who will evaluate the same experience differently. A splendid example of this is the remarkable experience of Saint Teresa of Avila called the Transverberation, a vision that has inspired a number of artistic masterpieces. First, let us read Saint Teresa's account of it.

> This time, though, the Lord desired that I see the vision in the following way: the angel was not large but small; he was very beautiful, and his face was so aflame that he seemed to be one of those very sublime angels that appear to be all afire. They must belong to those they call the cherubim, for they didn't tell me their names. But I see clearly that in heaven there is so much difference between some angels and others and between these latter and still others that I wouldn't know how to explain it. I saw in his hands a large golden dart and at the end of the iron tip there appeared to be a little fire. It seemed to me this angel plunged the dart several times into my heart and that it reached deep within me. When he drew it out, I thought he was carrying off with him the deepest part of me; and he left me all on fire with great love of God.[10]

[9] Anthony Bloom, *Beginning to Pray* (New York: Paulist Press, 1970), x–xii.

[10] Teresa of Avila, *Autobiography,* trans. Kavanaugh and Rodriguez, *Collected Works of St. Teresa of Avila,* vol. 1 (Washington, D.C.: ICS Publications, 1978), 193–94.

We can compare this autobiographical account with the evaluation of Saint John of the Cross who was writing on the fire of God's love. He obviously is referring to the experience of Saint Teresa and yet he seems to explain her vision as an attempt on her part (subconsciously) to deal in a conceptual way with the mystical graces she received.

> There is another way of cauterizing the soul by an intellectual form, usually very sublime, which is as follows. It will happen that while the soul is inflamed with the love of God, it will feel that a seraph is assailing it by means of an arrow or dart which is all afire with love. And the seraph pierces and cauterizes this soul which, like a red-hot coal, or better a flame, is already enkindled. And then in this cauterization, when the soul is transpierced with that dart, the flame gushes forth, vehemently and with a sudden ascent, like the fire in a furnace or an oven when someone uses a poker or bellows to stir and excite it. And being wounded by this fiery dart, the soul feels the wound with unsurpassable delight.[11]

I suggest that the reader who is edified by visions consider that sometimes a vision may be the individual's way of speaking and thinking about the unspeakable and unthinkable. We have no way of knowing where or how this process of transforming a spiritual reality into a psychic reality (an intellectual or imaginative vision) is taking place. Simply knowing this possibility makes it much easier to deal with many occasions of such experience from the lives of the saints of the past when visions were apparently much more commonplace than they are now.

[11] *The Living Flame of Love* in *The Complete Works of St. John of the Cross,* trans. Kavanaugh and Rodriguez (Washington, D.C.: ICS Publication, 1979), 598.

3. *Apparitions*. This word which is very much part of the vocabulary of devout Catholics is a general term and simply means an occasion when a presumably sane and sincere person reports "seeing and hearing" a heavenly visitor, usually the Blessed Virgin Mary. Usually no attempt is made in these cases to investigate whether the apparition is intellectual, imaginative, or external. Ordinarily only the alleged visionaries are able to see the apparition. In the rare case where there is a true supernatural phenomenon (equivalent to a miracle, i.e., a suspension of the laws of nature) it can be said to be an apparition, either in the form of an external or internal phenomenon not in any way caused by the individual who experiences it.

Saint Thomas Aquinas suggests that when the visionary alone sees the apparition it is subjective—that is within the inner functioning of the individual's mind.[12] In many cases we are reduced to mere conjecture as to how the apparition occurs.

Why So Many Reports of Apparitions?

Again conjecture is the best we can do. For those who are inclined to take all or most of these reports seriously, the most obvious explanation is that God through the Blessed Virgin is trying to warn the human race of impending disaster. Certainly the unstable world situation along with the incredible decline of morals would predispose the thoughtful to pause and ponder what is being said.

[12] Poulain, *Graces of Interior Prayer*, 315.

Another source of the thirst for apparitions is the damage done by skepticism on the part of religious personnel and teachers. Every time someone takes a hatchet to Scripture or Tradition in the name of organized religion the numbers of those who look for some other source of religious certitude grows. It is perhaps poetic justice that the very skeptics who cause religious anxiety and even panic are the ones most embarrassed by the devout who try to go directly to some presumed source of divine truth.

ADDENDUM
ON *A COURSE IN MIRACLES*

Those specifically interested in the *Course in Miracles* may find the following observations informative. Kenneth Wapnick, who was a close friend of Helen Schucman and mine, has written extensively on this book. Without going into many details I wish to take issue with two of his statements since I was known to be a friend of those involved.

Dr. Wapnick in an article in the *SCP Journal* (vol. 7, no. 1, p. 198) stated that he entered the Catholic Church only to become a monk. "I had no interest in the Catholic Church but I did have a strong intent in becoming a monk." If this was the case, the devout priest who baptized him (a confrere of mine, now deceased) and I were both deceived, and I continued to be deceived for a long time. Nothing in his behavior ever indicated to me that he was anything but a devout Catholic, careful to know and follow the specific teachings of the Catholic Church. When I became alarmed at the literal way people were taking the words of the *Course in Miracles,* I arranged for Dr. Wapnick to visit with a distinguished Jesuit theologian who is known for his orthodox views. The priest had carefully read the whole Course (something I never did) and pointed out that if one took it literally it contained several things against faith and even against reason. Dr. Wapnick engaged in this long meeting without ever indicating that he did not accept the teachings of the Church, although obviously he was not going to give up working on the Course. We talked for a long time immediately after leaving Saint Ignatius Loyola Church, and I implored Dr. Wapnick not to put his faith in anything as esoteric as the Course however beautiful parts of it might be. At no time did he mention any doubts about the Catholic Faith to me.

Secondly, contrary to Dr. Wapnick's statements, I recall that at least one time Helen Schucman believed herself actually to be a Catholic. When I informed her that she should formally apply to enter the Church (she had already been baptized as a young girl on her own impulse after visiting Lourdes), she dismissed the idea saying that her Jewish heritage made her automatically a member of the Church. "It was our religion first and you Gentiles came along and made all these rules later", she said with a laugh. She believed that so long as she accepted the Catholic Faith, she was automatically a member of the Church. As Dr. Wapnick pointed out she was a very conflicted person, but she seldom showed these conflicts to me. I had no recollection of her ever questioning any Catholic teaching except later those on birth control and some pro-life issues. From what Dr. Wapnick writes she apparently kept her feelings from me and from other Catholic friends. I personally never accepted the Course as a revelation of any kind. Because Dr. Wapnick appeared to be a devout Catholic, I hoped that both Helen and Dr. Thetford might follow him into the Church. This has proved to have been very naïve on my part, and I suspect reflects some of the confusion in Catholic religious circles in the beginning of the '70s.

Others have claimed that there is a diabolical element operating in this whole matter. At first this seemed to me to be very far-fetched. However, as I recall the terrible deterioration of Helen at the end of her life (she was frightening to be with) and her hatred for the Course and for all spiritual things, I have reason to wonder. When I see that devout people—both Christians and Jews—have replaced faith in divine revelation with this Course I am absolutely appalled. After apparently leaving the Church, Dr. Wapnick has written that this Course is not compatible with biblical Christianity (cf. *SCP* article). This contradicts what he originally believed because he did not take the Course literally. This whole matter highlights the necessity for being guided by the Church. Parts of the Course did help people, especially with forgiveness, but once it assumed authority beyond a piece of creative spiritual writing it became an obstacle to belief in revealed truth. I prayed that Dr. Wapnick would listen to the old Jesuit. I pray that now he and other followers of the Course will listen to the word of God and to the Church which Christ has given us to be our objective guide in this confusing world.

INDEX

Alacoque, St. Margaret
Mary. *See* Margaret
Mary Alacoque, St.
Angillara, Maria, 57
angry revelations, 84–86
Anne, St., 60
apparitions, 153, 157, 160–
61. *See also* Marian ap-
paritions; visions
approval, 28, 39–40, 99;
and disapproval, 41, 58–
59; and error, 29, 33, 95
Aquinas, St. Thomas, 160
arcana (secret knowledge),
118–19
Ascent of Mt. Carmel, The
(St. John of the Cross),
111n
Augustine, St., 83, 126,
136–37; *Confessions,*
136–37
authentic revelations, 31,
39–40, 91, 95; and error,
31, 49–53, 55–69, 71
automatic writing, 77, 155
automation, 119. *See also*
unconscious

Bahai faith, 20
Banneaux, 40
Bastien-Lepage, Jules, 52,
157
Beauraing, 40
Benedict XIV, Pope, 30,
55–56, 60n, 68, 109; on
approved revelations,
28, 29, 95
Benedict XIII (anti-pope),
103
Bernadette, St., 11, 37,
40–41, 97, 149; revela-
tion to, as inner, 51,
150, 155, 156; and hu-
man faith, 29, 30; and
interpretation, 32, 50;
revelation to, 130, 131;
scope of revelation to,
26, 33; simplicity of, 61,
137; testimony of, 42,
66, 93; virtues of, 113,
118
Bernanos, Georges, 85
Blavatsky, Helena, 98
Blessed Sacrament, 18, 24;
feast of, 112–13

32, 95, and extraordinary talent, 61–62; versus magic, 88–89; Oriental, 75; and private revelations, 23, 25

Naaman the leper, 123
Neubauer, Fr. Clement, 69
New Age movement, 13, 28; and *Course,* 83–84; and angry revelations, 85, 86; and paranormal phenomena, 11, 18
Nietzsche, Friedrich, 134

Oriental scriptures, 74–75
Our Lady of Mount Carmel, 55

Padre Pio, *See* Pio, Padre
papal teaching; on private revelations, 24, 27, 28, 30. *See also* Benedict XIV, Pope; John Paul II, Pope
Paprovick, Maria, 21
paramystical experiences, 11, 153–54; categories of, 154–60
paranormal phenomena, 11, 13, 18, 45–46, 97–99, 153–54. *See also* psychic phenomena
parapsychology, 32, 99, 112, 153–54, 155
patience, 112–13, 124

Paul, St., 13–14, 29–30, 122, 152, 154
Paul VI, Pope, 104
Peter, St., 13–14, 50
Peyramale, Abbé, 37
Pio, Padre, 68–69, 95, 98, 107, 154
Pisani, E., 58n
Pitra, Cardinal, 33
Pius XII, Pope *(Haurietis Aquas),* 30
Poem of the Man-God, The, 56–59
poor, 25, 125, 138–43, 146
Poulain, S. J., Fr. Augustin, 33, 42, 62, 77, 112, 157; on consulting visions, 63, 122; on errors, 51, 60n, 68; on false revelations, 44–45, 115–16, 119; *The Graces of Interior Prayer,* 12–13, 23, 78, 151; guidelines of, 23, 91, 103, 109, 110, 113, 122; on *Poem of the Man-God,* 57
private revelations, 19, 20–21, 25, 46–47; angry, 84–86; approved, 28, 29, 33, 39–40, 95, 99; authentic, 31, 39–40, 71, 91, 95; and Church, 25, 30, 32–33, 35, 36–37; dangers of, 55, 63, 118–19; description of, 25–26, 128; and error, 27–

28, 29, 31–34, 49–53,
55–69, 95; fraudulent,
39, 41–42, 43, 45–47,
91, 99–100; and holiness,
116–18; interest in, 17–
20, 125; mistrusting, 15,
121–22, 136, 150–51;
not directly from God,
27, 29, 31–33, 49–50;
obeying, 35–36, 113,
114–15; and paranormal
phenomena, 97–99; and
public revelation, 24–25;
questionable, 39, 40–42,
49, 56–59, 64–69; and
religious experience,
127–32; responding sen-
sibly to, 87, 91–106;
rules for, 21, 23–24, 27,
35, 49; and saints, 26,
27; scope of, 26, 33–34,
35–36. *See also* appari-
tions; false revelations;
locutions; public revela-
tion; visions
promises, 55–56
prophecy, 18, 34, 46, 153;
and assessing private
revelations, 28, 94, 103,
122
pseudomysticism, 18, 43,
46, 103
psychic phenomena, 18,
104, 153, 159. *See also*
paranormal phenomena
public revelation, 24–25,

29–30, 75; lack of error
in, 27, 29. *See also* Scripture; Tradition

questionable revelations,
39, 40–42, 49, 56–59,
64–69
questions for assessing
revelations, 93–97
quietism, 44, 79

Rahner, Karl, 25, 32
Rasputin, Grigori, 45, 98
Ratzinger, Cardinal
Joseph, 58n
religious experiences, 14–
15, 82, 125–47; available
to all, 132–33; definition
of, 151–52; examples of,
126–27, 129–30, 133–36,
136–37, 138–43, 143–46;
and false revelation, 74,
99–100; and private rev-
elations, 127–32. *See also*
extraordinary religious
experiences
revelation. *See* private revelations; public revela-
tions; Scripture;
Tradition
revelation addicts, 86–88
Ruffin, Bernard, 98
rules for private revela-
tions, 23–24; rule 1, 24–
26; rule 2, 27–34; rule 3,
35–37; rule 4, 49–69

unconscious, the, 28, 50,
81, 108, 119, 154
Underhill, Evelyn, 13, 81–
82, 88, 108–9, 119; *Mysticism*, 81–82
Under the Sun of Satan
(G. Bernanos), 85
Urban IV, Pope, 113
Ursula, St., 62

Valtorta, Maria, 56–59
Veronica of Binasco,
Blessed, 56
visions, 55, 109n, 150,
156–60; exterior, 156,
160; imaginative, 51–52,
64–65, 157, 159, 160;
inner, 51–52; intellec-
tual, 64–65, 157–59,
160. *See also* apparitions
von Speyr, Adrienne, 131–
32, 136, 152

Wapnick, Kenneth, 80,
163–65
Weible, Wayne, 67
Wolman, Dr. Benjamin,
99; *Handbook of Parapsychology*, 153
Wordsworth, William,
127

Zimdars-Swartz, Sandra,
17, 37, 42, 47, 67n
Zola, Émile, 101
Zolli, Rabbi, 152